WORLD WAR II
CARRIER WAR

Stephen W. Sears

AMERICAN HERITAGE • NEW WORD CITY

Published by New Word City, Inc.

For more information about New Word City, visit our Web site at
NewWordCity.com

American Heritage Publishing
Edwin S. Grosvenor, President
P.O. Box 1488
Rockville, MD 20851

1
THE DAY OF INFAMY

Hitokappu Bay, in the Kurile Islands north of Japan, is a cold and desolate place most of the year. It was particularly bleak in the gray light of dawn on November 26, 1941. The snow-covered shore was empty except for a concrete pier, a few fishermen's huts, and three tall radio masts swaying in the icy wind that swirled down from the surrounding mountains. In this unlikely setting, riding at anchor in the choppy waters of the bay, was the major striking power of the Imperial Japanese Navy.

In numbers, this task force was small - six aircraft carriers, two battleships, three cruisers, nine destroyers, and three submarines, with eight oil tankers for at-sea refueling - but in offensive power it was extremely strong. Nested aboard the big carriers were 423 warplanes, capable of swiftly reaching out hundreds of miles from their mobile "floating airfields" to smother a target with as much as 225 tons of bombs and aerial torpedoes. The thirty-one ships had arrived secretly, slipping out of various Japanese ports over a two-week period. All radio transmitters were shut down to prevent the tracing of messages.

On the bridge of the carrier *Akagi*, Vice Admiral Chuichi Nagumo, task force commander, issued an order. Signal flags fluttered from the flagship's yardarm. Winches hoisted rattling anchor chains, and steam turbines surged up to high speed. One by one the sleek gray ships put out to sea, shaping an easterly course across the foggy North Pacific.

In Washington, D.C., halfway around the world and on the other side of the International Date Line, it was early evening of the previous day, November 25. It had been a long and wearing day for officials of the American government. At noon, President Franklin D. Roosevelt had called together his chief advisers - Secretary of State Cordell Hull, Secretary of War Henry L. Stimson, Secretary of the Navy Frank Knox, the Navy's Admiral Harold R. Stark, the Army's General George C. Marshall - to discuss the growing crisis with Japan. As they weighed the chances of war breaking out in the Far East, the president reminded his advisers that "the Japanese are notorious for making an attack without warning." Returning to the War Department, Stimson learned that Japanese troop transports had been sighted sailing south along the China coast. He spoke to General Marshall and Admiral Stark about sending new warnings to American military commanders in the Pacific.

Prospects were dim for the United States remaining at peace much longer. World War II had broken out in Europe more than two years before. Adolf Hitler's German armies controlled most of the Continent and had driven deep into Russia. In North Africa, British forces were fighting hard against the Germans and their Italian allies, but at home, Britain was being bled white by submarine attacks on the merchant ships vital to its survival.

Refusing to stand idle in this world crisis, President Roosevelt proclaimed America the "Arsenal of Democracy" and ordered military supplies sent to both Britain and Russia. At the same time, the United States speeded up the painfully slow process of rearming after years of neglecting its military forces. While the Army and Navy suffered shortages of everything from medicine to machine guns, isolationists - those who insisted that America must stay out of the world's quarrels - loudly accused the president of pushing the nation toward war.

Roosevelt was walking a tightrope, trying to unite the country behind him in shoring up the nations fighting Nazi tyranny and at the same time trying to keep out of war until the armed forces were prepared to fight. His balancing act was made all the harder by Japan's threatening moves.

Since 1910, when they annexed Korea, the Japanese had been building an empire at their neighbors' expense. During World War I, they strengthened their position in Asia, and in 1931, they invaded Manchuria and began carving off pieces of China. By 1937, they were waging a full-scale war against the Chinese. The strongest force in Japan was not Emperor Hirohito and his government officials but an iron-willed group of Imperial Army officers known to its opponents as the Manchuria Gang. The goal of these ambitious warlords was nothing less than a vast empire in Asia and the southwest Pacific that would bring Japan unlimited natural resources and make her ruler of half of the world's population.

The Manchuria Gang saw the war that burst upon Europe in 1939 as a golden opportunity. By 1941, Japan had signed up with the other Axis powers, Germany and Italy, and was menacing the Asian possessions of France, the Netherlands, and Great Britain. The oil-rich Netherlands East Indies (now called Indonesia) was the prize most wanted by the Japanese.

These actions concerned and angered the American government. Secretary of State Cordell Hull told the

Japanese ambassador that the United States would not "sit absolutely quiet while two or three nations before our very eyes organized naval and military forces and went out and conquered the balance of the earth. "When Japanese soldiers completed their occupation of French Indochina in July of 1941, President Roosevelt reacted vigorously by "freezing" Japanese funds in the United States. Soon it was impossible for Japan to buy American oil, and the Netherlands East Indies followed the president's lead.

Roosevelt was playing a trump card in the grim game to halt Japanese aggression, for over 80 percent of Japan's oil came from these two sources. Only when the Imperial Army withdrew from Indochina and ended the fighting in China, said the president, would the flow of oil resume. For the warlords, this would mean humiliating "loss of face" and an end to their dreams of glory. Japan's diplomats were ordered to seek a peaceful settlement while the military put the finishing touches on plans for war. On October 17, 1941, tough, intense General Hideki Tojo, leader of the Manchuria Gang, became prime minister, the emperor's chief government official.

Japanese forces in French Indochina were strengthened, and armies were readied to strike at Singapore and Hong Kong, Britain's main outposts in Asia. Soldiers and planes were massed on the island of Formosa, less than 500 miles from American military bases in the Philippine Islands. And Admiral Nagumo's carrier task force, in complete secrecy, steamed out of Hitokappu Bay into the North Pacific.

On Wednesday, November 26, Secretary of War Stimson wrote in his diary that Roosevelt "fairly blew up" when he learned of the troop transports spotted off the China coast. Late that afternoon, Hull gave ambassadors Kichisaburo Nomura and Saburo Kurusu a strong statement that repeated American demands for an end to all Japanese aggression in Asia. The ambassadors were upset. Tokyo had given them until November 29 to reach an agreement with the United States; after that, the message warned mysteriously, "things are automatically going to happen." The deadline was only three days away, and the American leaders had not budged an inch.

The United States still had a trump card left, if a way could be found to play it. For more than a year, ever since Army Colonel William F. Friedman "broke" Japan's top-secret Purple Code, U.S. Intelligence officers had been able to read the messages Tokyo radioed to its diplomats all over the world. So the president was well aware that in a few days, important things, things that would probably mean war, were "automatically going to happen." Just where they would happen, however, the Purple Code did not reveal.

Most clues pointed toward the Far East; government leaders were sure that Japan would avoid a head-on collision with the United States and its enormous industrial strength if easier gains could be made in Asia. They were equally sure that the Japanese would have to throw all their military strength into any thrust southward toward the Netherlands East Indies.

Late the next day, November 27, warnings went out to U.S. Pacific outposts and the Panama Canal. The Army's message to General Douglas MacArthur at Manila in the Philippines said that diplomatic efforts were exhausted, with "hostile action possible at any moment." Even stronger was the Navy's message to Admiral Thomas C. Hart at Manila and to Admiral Husband E. Kimmel, commander of the U.S. Pacific Fleet at Pearl Harbor in the Hawaiian Islands. "This dispatch is to be considered a war warning," it began bluntly and went on to say that Southeast Asia, the Netherlands East Indies, or the Philippines would be the likeliest Japanese targets.

Admiral Hart reacted quickly, hurrying along his small fleet of cruisers, destroyers, and submarines to safer waters south of the Philippines. Radar warning stations and fighter plane squadrons guarding the Panama Canal went on full alert. At Pearl Harbor, the warning messages were received calmly. The Army's Lieutenant General

Walter C. Short double-checked his sabotage alert that guarded against possible attacks on military installations by the 158,000 people of Japanese descent living in the Hawaiian Islands. Admiral Kimmel went ahead with plans to send the aircraft carrier *Enterprise* with a load of fighter planes to reinforce the lonely U.S. outpost at Wake Island and continued the busy training schedules for the rest of the fleet based at Pearl Harbor.

As the various U.S. commanders took action on the warning messages from Washington, Admiral Nagumo's task force steamed on slowly across the North Pacific. The admiral was nervous about his mission, wondering if it might not be a terrible mistake. The whole idea of long-range carrier striking forces was still very new. He had confidence in his well-trained airmen and their planes, but he was also aware that he was risking all the Imperial Navy's large carriers.

The six carriers were at the center of the formation, flanked by the battleships and cruisers. Destroyers and submarines ranged out ahead to scout. They sighted nothing, and nothing sighted them. The only difficulty was refueling from the oil tankers. Several sailors were lost overboard in the rough seas, and the effort failed.

On Friday, November 28, the deciphered Purple Code brought Washington an interesting piece of information. Tokyo informed ambassadors

Nomura and Kurusu that diplomatic talks would soon be broken off; the ambassadors, however, were to pretend to keep trying for a settlement. The president ordered the State Department to prepare a message that he would send to Emperor Hirohito in a last effort to keep peace in the Pacific.

At Pearl Harbor that day, Vice Admiral William F. Halsey received final instructions from Admiral Kimmel before sailing aboard the *Enterprise* for Wake Island. Kimmel showed him the previous day's "war warning" from Washington. When he put to sea, Halsey ordered his scout pilots to attack any Japanese ship or plane they saw. His Operations officer was aghast: "Admiral, you can't start a private war of your own! Who's going to take the responsibility?"

"I'll take it," Halsey snapped. "If anything gets in my way, we'll shoot first and argue afterwards."

The weekend passed quietly. Aboard Nagumo's ships the crews grew restless and gossiped about where they were going. Some sailors thought they would turn south and strike at the Philippines. A pilot was sure the target would be in the north because the plane engines were equipped with winter oil. Refueling continued, with better success this time. No scout planes were launched for fear they would be seen by a passing ship.

In Washington, the first week of December began

on an ominous note. Reports from the Far East told of a flurry of Japanese military activity. Deciphered Purple Code messages revealed that Tokyo was ordering its ambassadors in major cities around the world to destroy their secret code books, something always done when war threatened.

Late Monday evening, a radio message was sent from Tokyo to Admiral Nagumo. It was not in code, and it simply said, "Climb Mount Niitaka." Although the phrase would mean nothing to American Intelligence if it was intercepted, Nagumo knew exactly what it meant: His government had made the final decision for war, and he would strike the first blow.

At Pearl Harbor on the following day, December 2, Admiral Kimmel and his Intelligence officer, Lieutenant Commander Edwin Layton, discussed the latest reports on the Imperial Japanese Navy. Layton was having problems. His radio operators listened in on the Japanese Navy's radio "traffic," and although they could not decipher the naval codes, they could at least identify and locate most of the ships by their radio call signs. On November 1, however, all call signs had been changed, and on December 1, they were changed again.

Layton had to report "almost a complete blank of information on the carriers today." Japan's largest aircraft carriers, in fact, had been "lost" for more than two weeks. This did not particularly worry

Admiral Kimmel, however. Intelligence often lost Japanese warships, especially when they were in their home ports and using different radio equipment. Only the day before, Naval Intelligence in Washington had reported that Japan's "major capital ship strength remains in home waters, as well as the greatest portion of the carriers."

Good news arrived that Tuesday from the Far East. Two of Great Britain's biggest warships, the battleship *Prince of Wales* and the battlecruiser *Repulse,* had arrived at Singapore. This was expected to make the Japanese think twice about causing trouble in Southeast Asia.

During the next few days, the American government marked time. A diplomatic stand had been taken. Military forces were alerted. All that remained was the president's personal appeal to Emperor Hirohito. If that failed, Roosevelt intended to draw a line and make it clear to the Japanese that if they stepped over the line, they risked war with the United States.

Nagumo's task force continued steaming eastward. The crews had finally been told where they were going, and airmen aboard the carriers carefully studied their target maps. On December 3, after more refueling, three of the tankers turned back. The fleet began to curve southward. Lookouts had yet to sight any American scouting planes or ships.

On the morning of Saturday, December 6, final refueling was completed, and every man not on duty assembled on the carrier flight decks. Up the *Akagi*'s mast went the flag flown in 1905 by the Japanese flagship at the Battle of Tsushima, a historic victory over the Russian Navy. Speeches were made, and a message from Tokyo read: "The moment has arrived. The rise or fall of the empire is at stake." Everyone cheered wildly. The remaining tankers faded out of sight far astern as the task force increased speed to twenty-six knots, driving hard on a southerly course.

At Pearl Harbor that Saturday, nearly half of the more than 200 ships of the Pacific Fleet were in port, including eight of its nine battleships. Among the ships absent on training maneuvers or special missions, however, were all three of the fleet's aircraft carriers and their escorts of cruisers and destroyers. The *Saratoga* was at sea off San Diego, California; a task force built around the *Lexington* had left the previous day to deliver fighter planes to Midway Island; and Halsey's *Enterprise* task force was returning from Wake. The *Enterprise* crew was unhappy because bad weather had delayed them a day and they would arrive on the seventh, missing the pleasures of Saturday night in port. On the Army's airfields around Pearl Harbor, the planes were parked close together to be easily guarded against sabotage. Many of them had their guns out for cleaning.

It was a busy Saturday evening in Washington. By 9:00 p.m., the president's message to Emperor Hirohito was on its way. It reviewed recent events in the Far East and warned that the people of Asia could not "sit either indefinitely or permanently on a keg of dynamite." It was his "fervent hope," Roosevelt said, "that Your Majesty may, as I am doing, give thought in this definite emergency to ways of dispelling the dark clouds."

That evening, Intelligence decoded a long Purple Code message sent from Tokyo to ambassadors Nomura and Kurusu, and by 9:30, it was in the president's hands. The final part of the message was not due to arrive until the following morning, but it was clear that Japan was breaking off diplomatic talks. Roosevelt turned to one of his advisers, Harry Hopkins, and said quietly, "This means war." Hopkins replied that it was too bad "we could not strike the first blow and prevent any sort of surprise."

"No, we can't do that," the president said, "We are a democracy and a peaceful people."

Early the next morning, Sunday, December 7, the final part of the message from Tokyo arrived in Washington and was decoded. As expected, Japan was ending diplomatic talks. A Navy officer, Lieutenant Commander A. D. Kramer, delivered this to key government officials. When he returned to his office, Kramer found a second Purple Code item. It told the Japanese ambassadors to deliver the entire message to Secretary of State Hull at exactly 1:00 p.m. Washington time, two and a half hours away.

Kramer was startled. Japan was not only ending negotiations but was ordering its ambassadors precisely when to tell the American government this piece of news. Wondering if the message was actually a cunning way to declare war, Kramer quickly made some time calculations. One p.m. December 7 in Washington was 1:30 a.m. December 8 in Singapore and just a half hour later in the Philippines. But at Pearl Harbor, it would be 7:30 a.m. December 7 - early Sunday morning, the perfect time for a surprise attack.

Admiral Stark read the new message immediately, but forty-five minutes passed before it was seen by General Marshall, who had been taking his regular Sunday morning horseback ride. After he and Stark talked over the one o'clock deadline, Marshall wrote out a warning for all Pacific commanders. He mentioned the deadline and added, "Just what significance the hour set may have we do not know, but be on the alert . . ."

Because of heavy static, Pearl Harbor could not be reached directly by radio from Washington. The message was sent by telegraph to California and then on to Hawaii. The War Department message center failed to mark it urgent, and it reached Pearl Harbor in midafternoon.

While General Marshall was writing out his warning, Admiral Nagumo's carriers were turning into the wind to launch planes. It was 6:00 a.m., and the sun was just coming up as one after another the first wave of attack planes roared down the flight decks. First off were forty-three Zero fighters, followed by fifty-one Val dive bombers carrying 750-pound bombs. Last came eighty-nine Kate torpedo bombers. The planes assembled in formation over the carriers and then headed due south for the Hawaiian island of Oahu. Their target, Pearl Harbor, was less than two hours flying time away.

It was a typically peaceful Sunday morning at Pearl Harbor. The morning watch aboard the warships went about its usual duties. The dawn patrol of three Navy Catalina flying boats was tracing a search pattern west of Oahu. There were no Army fighter patrols in the air.

Suddenly, two miles outside the entrance to the harbor, was a commotion. The destroyer *Ward*, on morning patrol, sighted and sank what was later identified as a small Japanese submarine, and reported the sinking to naval headquarters at Pearl Harbor just before 7:00 a.m. After considerable delay, key officers were reached, and they tried to get more information about the action. At 7:40, Admiral Kimmel was called. He said he would come to headquarters immediately.

Army headquarters had meanwhile received an unusual telephone call. The operators of a radar station on the northern tip of Oahu called at 7:20 to report "a large number of planes coming in from the north." The radarmen were excited; they had never before seen such a big "blip" on their screen. The young officer at headquarters was new to his job and decided that the planes must be Flying Fortress heavy bombers scheduled to arrive from California that morning. "Don't worry about it," he told the radar operators.

At 7:55 Sunday morning, December 7, 1941, the fragile peace between the United States and Japan was shattered. A Japanese Val dive bomber screamed down, and its bomb hit the seaplane ramp on Ford Island in the center of Pearl Harbor. A minute later, Kates put torpedoes into the light cruisers Raleigh and Helena and the target ship Utah. Other Kates came skimming low across the harbor, heading straight for the line of battleships moored like sitting ducks alongside Ford Island.

Aboard the battleship, Nevada the flag was being raised and the ship's band was playing "The Star-Spangled Banner" when a Kate flashed by overhead. The rear gunner fired his machine gun at the band and missed; the musicians did not skip a beat. Torpedoes churned through the water while crewmen aboard the ships rushed for alarm bells. Great fountains of water erupted next to the battleships as the torpedoes struck: one into the *Nevada;* two each into the *California* and the *Arizona;* five into the *Oklahoma;* six into the *West Virginia.* It reminded an eyewitness of an expert bowler throwing one strike after another.

The fleet's antiaircraft guns were quickly manned, but only a quarter of them were loaded. Sailors smashed the doors off ammunition lockers in their desperate haste to fight back. They had plenty of targets, for now dive bombers joined in the attack on "Battleship Row."

The *Tennessee* and the *Maryland,* shielded by other ships, suffered no torpedo hits, but both were damaged by bombs. Water poured into great rents in the *California's* side, oil from her fuel tanks burst into flame, and she gradually settled. The *West Virginia* began to heel over sharply, but well-trained crewmen flooded compartments on the opposite side, and the ship sank evenly onto the bottom of the shallow harbor.

The crew of the *Oklahoma* had no time for counter-flooding, and within eight minutes, the battleship rolled over and sank with the loss of 415 men. The *Arizona* suffered an even worse fate. In addition to two torpedoes, she was hit by eight bombs. One of them ripped deep into the hull and went off in an ammunition magazine. The enormous explosion broke the *Arizona* in half, killing 1,100 men.

As the devastation of Battleship Row continued, other Japanese planes concentrated on knocking out American airpower on Oahu. Their attacks were carried out with precision and skill, and their victory was all but complete.

At the Naval Air Station on Ford Island, Val dive bombers shattered the thirty-three fighters and bombers lined up on the runway. Vals and Zero fighters made equally short work of every Catalina flying boat at the Navy's nearby seaplane base. The Marine field failed to get a single plane into the air in the face of severe bombing and low-level strafing by Zeros. At Hickam Field, the Army's bomber base, one plane after another went up in flames.

Wheeler Field, the Army's main fighter base, was given special attention by the Japanese. Sixty-two of the Army's new P-40 fighters were parked wingtip to wingtip in neat rows. In spite of the gallant efforts of pilots and mechanics firing rifles and machine guns, most of the grounded fighters were shot to pieces.

Almost the only success the Army had that grim day was furnished by two fighter pilots. Lieutenants Kenneth Taylor and George Welch. Their P-40s were stationed at a small airfield the Japanese apparently did not know about, and they managed to take off and get into the fight. First they raced for Hickam Field and shot down two strafing Zeros. When they ran out of targets there, they shifted to the Marine airfield, under attack by Val dive bombers. The Vals were easy pickings, and before they ran out of ammunition, Taylor and Welch added five more enemy planes to their bag.

In the midst of the attack, the B-17 Flying Fortresses expected from California arrived right on schedule. All the big bombers managed to make safe but hair-raising landings. Scout planes flying to Ford Island from the carrier *Enterprise,* then 200 miles west of Oahu, were also caught in the surprise attack. Several were shot down by Japanese fighters, and others were riddled by American antiaircraft gunners who were firing at anything that flew across their gunsights.

At about 8:30 a.m., the first wave of Japanese planes finished its job and headed back to the carriers. Fifteen minutes later a second wave of 170 bombers and fighters appeared over Pearl Harbor. The pilots pressed home their attacks through huge columns of black smoke from the burning ships in Battleship Row.

One target was the battleship *Pennsylvania,* tied up in a dry dock along with two destroyers. A civilian Navy Yard worker ran his big crane back and forth on the dock alongside the ships in a courageous effort to distract the enemy pilots. The battleship was only slightly damaged, but the two destroyers took a fearful pounding.

No event of that terrible Sunday morning buoyed up the embattled Americans at Pearl Harbor so much as the gallant sortie of the battleship *Nevada*. She had been hit by a torpedo in the first minutes of the battle, but accurate antiaircraft fire drove off the majority of later attackers. The *Nevada* was the only battleship that had any steam up at all; just as the second wave of enemy planes appeared, she began to move slowly and majestically past Battleship Row.

An *Enterprise* pilot, who had bailed out of his plane after it was hit by Zeros, watched from the shore as the *Nevada* fought for her life. "Anywhere you looked her guns were going," he wrote. "Along the deck I saw wounded and men with stretchers were rushing to carry them away. . . . There was a tremendous ear-splitting explosion. A bomb had struck on her deck close to one of her antiaircraft guns. . . . Some were killed, more were hurt, but only one gun had stopped firing." It was clear that the Japanese dive bombers were trying to sink the battleship in the narrow channel, bottling up the rest of the fleet within the harbor, so she was run aground near the harbor mouth.

It was now after nine o'clock. Japanese fighters and bombers prowled over the whole Pearl Harbor area, dropping bombs on the likeliest targets and then shooting up their machine-gun ammunition at ships, grounded planes, Army barracks, cars, and even individual soldiers and sailors caught out in the open. The light cruiser *Raleigh* was hit by a bomb that went completely through her hull and exploded on the harbor bottom. Undaunted, the *Raleigh's* gunners claimed five enemy planes.

By 10:00 a.m., the last Japanese planes had headed north for their carriers. In the space of two hours, Admiral Nagumo's attack had killed 2,335 American servicemen, crippled the Battle Force of the Pacific Fleet, and virtually demolished U.S. air power in the Hawaiian Islands. Nagumo lost twenty-nine planes and fifty-five men. Aircraft carriers had delivered one of the greatest surprises in military history.

The electrifying news had reached Washington only minutes after the first bomb fell. A message from Admiral Kimmel was delivered to Secretary of the Navy Frank Knox: "Air raid on Pearl Harbor. This is no drill." Turning to Admiral Stark, Knox exclaimed, "My God, this can't be true! This must mean the Philippines!" "No, sir," Stark said grimly, "this is Pearl."

Shortly after noon the next day, President Franklin Roosevelt stood before Congress to ask for a declaration of war against the Axis powers. He spoke in measured tones: "Yesterday, December 7, 1941 - a date which will live in infamy - the United States of America was suddenly and deliberately attacked by naval and air forces of the Empire of Japan. . . ."

America was at war at last. And it was a united, purposeful, furious America, armed with a ringing battle cry – "Remember Pearl Harbor!"

2
"HIT THEM WHEN YOU CAN"

A	t dusk on December 8, 1941, the carrier *Enterprise* and her escort of cruisers and destroyers slipped into Pearl Harbor. Officers and men lined the rails, watching in stunned silence the scene of devastation that unfolded as they steamed up the channel. Wrecked planes littered the runways of Hickam Field. The twisted, smoldering superstructure of the *Arizona* glowed redly, and there was a stench of charred wood and fuel oil in the air.

"Morale went to nothing just about then," said an officer on one of the escorting cruisers. "We weren't frightened - or maybe we were. But we certainly were sick and shocked. We couldn't believe that this had happened to us." Through the night, Admiral

Halsey's task force took on fuel, provisions, and ammunition, and before dawn it was back at sea.

The *Enterprise's* quick stopover underlined two important facts about the surprise attack of December 7: The Pacific Fleet's carriers were intact and ready for action, and Pearl Harbor still functioned as a fleet base. The Japanese raiders had ignored docks and repair shops, as well as storage tanks holding over 140 million gallons of fuel oil. Even the tanker *Neosho,* loaded with high-test aviation gasoline and anchored in the middle of Battleship Row, was not hit.

The fact remained, however, that at Pearl Harbor, the United States had suffered a humiliating blow. Half a dozen investigations were held to find out what had happened and why surprise had been complete. Scores of witnesses were heard, and thousands of documents were studied, and all the steps that led up to that fatal Sunday were carefully analyzed. Under this mountain of evidence lay the simple fact that American military and government leaders had underestimated the enemy's war machine and badly misjudged its intentions. To add to the humiliation, it was soon clear that Pearl Harbor was only the first of a series of moves on Japan's military chessboard.

The Pearl Harbor attack had been planned with one purpose in mind: to make sure that the Pacific Fleet would not interfere with Japan's timetable of conquest in the Far East. Tojo and his warlords had to have the oil of the Netherlands East Indies, but they also needed tin, rubber, rice, and bauxite (aluminum ore) from the Indies and Southeast Asia. Their strategy called for a lightning offensive to seize these resources, followed by the building of a ring of defenses strong enough to beat off any counterattacks. Speed was the key to this plan. "I can raise havoc with them for one year," Admiral Isoroku Yamamoto, commander in chief of the Imperial Navy, told his government, "but after that I can give no guarantee."

Within four hours after the last of Admiral Nagumo's carrier planes left Pearl Harbor, Japanese bombers raided the British strongholds of Hong Kong and Singapore and the American-held Pacific islands of Guam and Wake. Four hours after that, bombers and fighters from Formosa wrecked half of General MacArthur's planes in the Philippines.

The Japanese rolled southward with the speed and power of an avalanche. On December 10, Guam fell, and the Philippines were invaded. The same day, Britain's battleship *Prince of Wales* and the battle cruiser *Repulse* were attacked by Japanese bombers 125 miles from Singapore. Both ships were torn apart by bombs and torpedoes and sent to the bottom.

On December 23, after a heroic defense by U.S. Marines, Wake Island fell to an invading force. On

Christmas Day, the British surrendered Hong Kong. On January 2, 1942, Japanese troops entered Manila, capital of the Philippines, driving MacArthur's troops into the Bataan peninsula. By mid-January, enemy forces were nearing Singapore and had won footholds in the Netherlands East Indies.

As the grim news poured in from the Pacific, the U.S. Navy took stock of its situation. One of the first acts was to replace Admiral Kimmel as head of the Pacific Fleet. Even though many others shared with him the blame for the Pearl Harbor surprise, Kimmel, along with General Short, was branded with the defeat. On December 17, 1941, Admiral Chester W. Nimitz was named commander of the Pacific Fleet.

Nimitz was a calm, patient, fifty-six-year-old Texan, known as an able strategist and an excellent judge of men. He arrived at Pearl Harbor Christmas Day and took over his new duties on the last day of the year. That same day, Admiral Ernest J. King, another man who would put his stamp on the course of the war, became commander in chief of the United States Fleet. It would have been hard to find anyone who looked more the part of a fleet commander than Ernest King. He was tall, ramrod-straight, outspoken, and forbidding; it was said, only half in jest, that he shaved with a blowtorch. King had been forty years in the Navy, was qualified as a naval aviator, and for two years had been captain of the carrier *Lexington*. He was considered a skilled student of carrier warfare.

As naval historian, Samuel Eliot Morison wrote, King's main problem was that he "had a two-ocean war to wage with a less than one-ocean Navy." Overall war policy called for a Germany-first strategy. The Nazi menace was considered the most immediate threat to the free world, and so the war in Europe had first call on America's military resources. This meant that in the Pacific, at least during 1942, the United States would have to follow a defensive-offensive strategy. Such a strategy, wrote King, "may be paraphrased as 'hold what you've got and hit them when you can,' the hitting to be done not only by seizing opportunities but by making them."

Already American submarines were prowling deep into enemy waters after Japanese warships, tankers, and merchantmen. To carry out King's orders to hold and hit, however, Admiral Nimitz had to depend primarily on his aircraft carriers. He dared not risk an old-fashioned big-gun sea battle, for the battleships left to him after the Pearl Harbor attack were too old, too slow, and too few in number to challenge the Imperial Navy. Until these old battleships were modernized and new ones then under construction arrived, carrier task forces were the only weapons in the Navy's arsenal that could do what needed to be done - strike fast and hard at the enemy, fade away into the broad Pacific, and pop up the next day hundreds of miles away to strike again.

The U.S. Navy had seven large fleet carriers and one small escort carrier at the outbreak of war. The *Lexington* and the *Saratoga* were the biggest and the oldest, having joined the fleet in 1927. They were rugged, powerful ships of 33,000 tons, originally laid down as battle cruisers. The Ranger, designed from the keel up as a carrier, was completed in 1934, and between 1937 and 1941, *Yorktown, Enterprise,* Wasp, *Hornet,* and the escort carrier *Long Island* joined the fleet.

The Imperial Navy also received its first fleet carrier, the *Akagi,* in 1927. The Japanese stepped up carrier construction in the late 1930s, and by December of 1941, they had six fleet and four light carriers, an edge of ten to eight over the U.S. Navy.

The typical American or Japanese carrier of the time had a wooden flight deck. Below this was the hangar deck, extending almost the full length of the ship, where planes were stored and serviced. Elevators carried them to and from the flight deck. Deep in the hull were bomb, torpedo, and ammunition magazines and tanks for fuel oil and aviation gasoline. Oil-fired boilers provided steam for great turbines that turned up speeds as high as thirty knots or more. Carriers depended on their speed, their fighter planes, and their antiaircraft guns for defense, for they had little armor and were very vulnerable to fire.

An American fleet carrier (CV in naval terminology) had as many as 2,900 crewmen and seventy to ninety planes, divided into fighter, torpedo bomber, and scout-dive bomber squadrons. Early in the war, most U.S. squadrons were numbered according to the carrier they served on. Fighting 2, for example, was the fighter squadron aboard the *Lexington* (CV-2); Torpedo 7 was the torpedo bomber squadron of the *Wasp* (CV-7). Most of the Japanese fleet carriers had smaller crews and fewer planes.

The standard U.S. carrier fighter was the chubby Grumman F4F Wildcat. It was outperformed in most flight characteristics by the Imperial Navy's lighter and faster Zero, but it could hit harder and take more hits than the agile Japanese fighter. Wildcat pilots quickly discovered that the Zero, for all its flashy performance, was likely to disintegrate if caught in the heavy firepower of the F4F's six .50-caliber machine guns.

The Douglas TBD Devastator torpedo bomber was far outclassed by Japan's Kate and was a deathtrap for a good many American airmen until it was replaced in mid-1942. On the other hand, the Japanese Val dive bomber was inferior to the Douglas SBD Dauntless. The Dauntless was a good scout plane and a superb dive bomber.

Early in 1942, the *Yorktown* joined *Lexington, Enterprise,* and *Saratoga* in the Pacific, and the four carriers became sentinels for the Hawaiian Islands and shepherds for troop convoys sent to keep open the lifeline to Australia. On January 11, a Japanese submarine put a torpedo into the *Saratoga,* forcing her to return to the United States for repairs. Nevertheless, Admiral Nimitz went ahead with a limited offensive.

The same day that the *Saratoga* was torpedoed, Admiral Halsey's *Enterprise* task force left Pearl Harbor. His orders were to swing south to oversee the landing of troops in the Samoa Islands and then turn northward to raid the Japanese-held Marshall and Gilbert islands. He would be joined at Samoa by the *Yorktown* task force. Rear Admiral Frank Jack Fletcher commanding.

The *Enterprise* had a long way to go to reach her target, and most of the time was spent in drills. Dive bomber pilots practiced their trade by aiming dummy bombs at a big mat towed behind one of the escort ships. Antiaircraft gunners improved their aim by blazing away at shellbursts from the 5-inch guns. Every day at dawn and dusk, the most likely times of attack, the call to general quarters sent the crews running to battle stations.

Misfortune seemed to follow the task force. On January 16, for example, an explosion in a gun turret killed a sailor on the cruiser *Salt Lake City,* and a second man died in a landing accident aboard the *Enterprise*. That afternoon, a Devastator failed to return from patrol duty. When search planes failed to locate any sign of the torpedo bomber, Halsey reluctantly marked the crew missing and presumed dead and ordered the task force to continue on.

The three crewmen of the Devastator, however, were very much alive. Out of fuel and unable to locate the carrier. Chief Machinist Mate Harold Dixon had skillfully "ditched" the heavy plane in the ocean. Dixon, bombardier Tony Pastula, and gunner Gene Aldrich had just time enough to inflate their rubber life raft before the Devastator sank. Their possessions included a penknife, a pistol, an empty water bottle, a length of rope, two pairs of pliers, and the clothes they wore. They had no food or water.

Dixon estimated that the nearest land lay hundreds of miles to the southeast. Wise in the ways of navigation after twenty-two years in the Navy, he set a course as best he could. With a favorable wind, they made thirty or forty miles a day. When the wind was against them, Dixon held their position with a crude sea anchor made from a life jacket and a rope. When there was no wind at all, they used their shoes as paddles.

The constant pounding of the waves on the four-by-eight-foot raft almost drove the three men out of their minds. As Dixon described it,

"Imagine doubling up on a tiny mattress, with the strongest man you know striking the underside as hard as he could with a baseball bat, twice every three seconds, while someone else hurls buckets of cold salt water in your face. That's what it was like."

As the days passed, the tortures of thirst, hunger, sun, and salt water strained their endurance to the breaking point. Their only food was two fish, a small shark, two seabirds - all of which they killed with the gun or the penknife and ate raw - and two coconuts that drifted near enough for them to reach. An occasional rain squall kept them from dying of thirst. Twice, storms capsized the raft. On the thirty-second day, they capsized again, losing everything. The raft now drifted aimlessly. The men hardly had the strength to move, and they fell into periods of delirium.

At midmorning on the thirty-fourth day, as the raft topped the crest of a wave, Aldrich exclaimed, "Chief, I see a beautiful field of corn... Sure enough, Chief! I see something in the distance!"

A few hours later, the men staggered ashore on Pukapuka near the Society Islands, 750 miles from the spot where their plane had gone down. The next day, they were found by friendly natives who nursed them back to health. Later, they were rescued by a destroyer and taken to Pearl Harbor to be decorated for "extraordinary heroism" by Admiral Nimitz.

While Dixon and his crew waged their fight for life, their shipmates were going into action. Before dawn on February 1, the *Enterprise's* crew was called to duty. The airmen gathered in their ready rooms to be briefed on their mission. The targets were airfields and military installations in the Marshall Islands, with the best pickings expected at Kwajalein. They were also briefed on radio call signs, weather, and navigation data, such as where the carrier would be upon their return.

Shortly before 4:30 a.m., the fliers manned their planes. The "Big E" turned head-on into the wind at 30 knots as the signal was given to start engines. The pilot of the lead SBD tramped on his brakes, revved up his engine, and received the takeoff signal. The Dauntless leaped down the dark flight deck between rows of hooded lights. As soon as it was airborne, a second SBD surged forward.

After thirty-seven dive bombers and nine Devastator torpedo bombers had taken off, six Wildcats were sent aloft to form a protective combat air patrol over the task force. The bombers headed westward to make the first American offensive strike of World War II.

It was 7:00 a.m. when they swooped down on their island targets. The surprised Japanese gunners began blazing away at the intruders. The action took place in the first glow of dawn, and to SBD pilot Clarence Dickinson there was a spectacular and deadly beauty about it. "Great white and pinkish streaked fire shapes bloomed profusely, each for just an instant," Dickinson wrote. "The bombs went off in big bluish flashes two and two and two each time another plane glided in. Those bomb explosions were fiercely jagged, intensely bright."

At Kwajalein, the airmen of Bombing 6 and Torpedo 6 sank a big transport and a patrol craft and damaged nine other ships, including a light cruiser. Admiral Fletcher was less fortunate in his attacks on other Japanese bases in the Marshalls and Gilberts that day. His *Yorktown* planes were hampered by bad weather and did little damage.

When the raiders returned, the *Enterprise* again turned into the wind, and the planes formed a landing circle around her. One by one, with wheels, wing flaps, and tail hooks down, they came in over the stern. The landing officer standing on a platform at the left rear corner of the flight deck guided the pilots into the landing "groove" by wigwagging colored paddles. As each plane settled down, arrester wires stretched across the deck caught its tail hook and jerked it to a stop. Deckmen quickly released the hook, the pilot taxied forward to park, and the next plane came in to land.

The Big E was withdrawing at top speed when she had the dubious honor of being the first American carrier to face air attack. The land-based Japanese bombers were badly mauled by Wildcats of the combat air patrol and scored no hits. The pilot of one crippled bomber, however, determined to make a death dive into the *Enterprise*. Despite a hail of antiaircraft fire, he doggedly pursued his quarry.

Just then a mechanic named Bruno Gaido jumped into a Dauntless parked at the rear edge of the flight deck and began hammering away at the diving bomber with the twin guns in the SBD's rear cockpit. At the last second, the bomber faltered, bounced on the edge of the flight deck, tore off the tail of Gaido's SBD, and slid overboard. The triumphant Gaido swiveled his guns downward and poured a final burst into the sinking wreckage.

With one reasonably successful raid behind them, the U.S. carriers set out on further hit-and-run strikes at the fringes of Japan's empire. The *Enterprise* pounded the islands of Wake and Marcus in the Central Pacific while the *Lexington* and the *Yorktown* ranged deep into enemy waters south of the equator.

None of these carrier raids did major harm to the enemy – "the Japs didn't mind them any more than a dog minds a flea," was how one American officer put it - but they did provide excellent combat training. Airmen were able to hone their skills in the most effective way - against a live enemy - and commanders gained knowledge about handling and supplying task forces thousands of miles from their home bases. Equally important, the attacks were some small comfort to American civilian morale, which just then was near rock bottom.

During January and February 1942, German submarines sank more than 100 Allied merchant ships in the Atlantic. In the Far East, Japan broke the last defenses of the Netherlands East Indies, took the British fortress of Singapore, and conquered Burma. General MacArthur was ordered out of the Philippines, and on April 9, his forces on Bataan surrendered. Corregidor Island, the last American foothold in the Philippines, held out a month longer. For the moment, the Japanese were masters of all they surveyed in Asia and the western Pacific.

The last of these early U.S. carrier strikes was the most spectacular and important. On April 2, 1942, the carrier *Hornet* steamed out of San Francisco Bay with sixteen twin-engine Army B-25 bombers perched on her flight deck. Also aboard to fly them was a group of Army airmen led by Lieutenant Colonel Jimmy Doolittle. Before the war, Doolittle had captured many flying records and a long list of air races and was perhaps the best-known pilot in the world. His assignment was to bomb Japan.

The notion of bombing the Japanese homeland was the brainchild of one of Admiral King's assistants, Captain Francis S. Low. The aircraft carrier was the only available "platform" from which to launch such a raid, yet ordering a carrier in close enough to Japan to send off her planes would just about guarantee her destruction. Low's idea was to use long-range B-25s so that the carrier could launch a good deal farther away and escape detection. The trouble was that no one knew whether a B-25, which was three times as heavy as the biggest carrier plane, could take off from a carrier. There was only one way to find out. In February, off Norfolk, Virginia, Army pilots flew two B-25s off the *Hornet* with flight deck to spare.

From San Francisco, the *Hornet* steamed into the North Pacific and was joined by the *Enterprise*. The Big E's job was to provide air cover, for the bombers crowded on the *Hornet*'s deck prevented her from launching her own planes. The task force, under Bill Halsey's command, was to close to within 500 miles of Japan to launch the B-25s, which would land in China after bombing Tokyo and other major cities.

On April 18, the task force was still 650 miles from Japan when it was sighted by an enemy patrol boat. Halsey dared not risk the carriers any further, and Doolittle agreed that it was now or never. Shortly before 8:30 a.m., Doolittle gunned the first B-25 into the air. The other fifteen planes followed him off without mishap.

The patrol boat had radioed a warning, but Japanese defense officials assumed they had plenty of time to prepare before the carriers reached the point where they could launch any planes. As a result,

Doolittle's attack was a complete surprise. All the bombers hit their targets - one of which was an aircraft carrier under construction - and got away.

The early takeoff, however, left the raiders with too little fuel to land safely in China. In darkness and bad weather, fifteen of the bombers either crash-landed or were abandoned in the air as their crews bailed out. The remaining B-25 landed in Vladivostok, Russia; since the Russians were not at war with Japan, its crew was interned for a year before being released. Doolittle and most of his men found their way into friendly hands in China, but eight airmen were captured by the Japanese. Three were executed, and a fourth died of starvation in a Japanese prison.

What Admiral Halsey called "one of the most courageous deeds in all military history" gave a tremendous boost to American morale and a sharp jolt to Japan's warlords. They had pledged that the homeland would never be touched by war; now, just over four months after the beginning of the conflict, the capital itself had been bombed - exactly how, they were not quite sure. They finally concluded that the B-25s had been launched from a carrier, and they determined that an all-out attempt must be made to draw the U.S. fleet into a finish fight. This decision was to have a far-reaching effect on the course of the Pacific war.

Admiral Nagumo's carriers had covered a great deal

of ocean since Pearl Harbor. They had furnished air strikes in the invasion of Wake Island, in the seizure of the key base of Rabaul in the Bismarck Archipelago, and in the Netherlands East Indies campaign. Their most notable feat had been a sortie into the Indian Ocean, where they had sunk the British carrier *Hermes*, two cruisers, two destroyers, and assorted merchant ships.

In four months, Nagumo had bagged a huge score of enemy ships without the slightest damage to his own vessels. Yet the most important game, Nimitz's carriers, had eluded him. In early May 1942, hoping to remedy this situation, the Imperial Navy set about baiting a trap.

It was important for the Japanese to prevent Australia from becoming a jumping-off place for any counterattack on their newly won empire in the southwest Pacific. If they could seize bases at Tulagi in the Solomon Islands and at Port Moresby, near the eastern tip of New Guinea, they would have a good start at cutting Australia's lifeline to the United States.

On May 3, Tulagi was taken, and an invasion convoy moved toward Port Moresby. Covering these moves, and hoping to trap any U.S. carriers that tried to interfere, was a task force built around the Zuikaku and the Shokaku, the newest Japanese carriers. The U.S. Navy did, indeed, plan to interfere. Admiral Frank Jack Fletcher's Task

Force 17 the *Lexington*, the *Yorktown*, and a screen of cruisers and destroyers - steamed into the Coral Sea looking for trouble. On May 4, *Yorktown* planes raided Tulagi; the next day Task Force 17 pushed on to Port Moresby.

On May 6, the Japanese carrier task force entered the Coral Sea. Throughout the day, the two fleets groped for information, neither finding the other, neither even knowing the other was in the immediate area. At one point, only seventy miles separated them.

The Battle of the Coral Sea opened early on the morning of May 7 when a Japanese scout plane reported sighting an American carrier and a cruiser. Rear Admiral Tadaichi Hara immediately launched a seventy-eight-plane strike force at these tempting targets. To his chagrin, the "cruiser" turned out to be the destroyer *Sims* and the "carrier" the tanker *Neosho*. The *Sims* went down immediately under a hail of bombs. The *Neosho*, which had narrowly escaped destruction at Pearl Harbor on December 7 burned fiercely but was kept afloat for four days until her crew was rescued.

While Hara's planes were thus occupied, Admiral Fletcher launched an attack of his own. His scout planes had sighted the Japanese light carrier *Shoho*, sailing with the Port Moresby invasion force. A total of ninety-three planes from the *Lexington* and the *Yorktown* found the hapless carrier and tore her apart.

The leader of the *Yorktown*'s fighters, Lieutenant Commander James Flatley, reported that "the sight of those heavy bombs smashing that carrier was so awful it gave me a sick feeling. . . . She burst into flames from bow to stern. I don't see how anybody aboard that ship could have survived." As the *Shoho* went down, a radio report by Dauntless pilot Robert Dixon sent cheers ringing through the *Lexington:* "Scratch one flattop! Dixon to carrier. Scratch one flattop!"

The aggressive Admiral Hara wanted revenge, and that evening he dispatched twenty-seven bombers to try to locate Fletcher's carriers. As they searched in vain, they were tracked on the carriers' radar, and nine were "splashed" by Wildcats. Another was shot down when it mistook the *Yorktown* for its own carrier and tried to land; eleven more crashed on the return flight. Hara had lost twenty-one planes and gained nothing at all.

After two days of narrow misses, the opposing task forces finally came to grips on the morning of May 8. Soon after 8:00 a.m., both Japanese and American scout planes reported sightings, and both Hara and Fletcher launched air strikes. Some three hours later, *Yorktown* Dauntlesses bore down on the *Shokaku.* Two bombs tore open her flight deck, and a third hit was later scored by a *Lexington* plane.

The *Zuikaku* hid in a rain squall and was not attacked.

Both task forces landed their Sunday punches at almost the same time. The combat air patrol defending the American carriers was poorly directed, and only a handful of fighters were in position to meet Hara's raiders. The job of defense fell to the antiaircraft gunners. War correspondent Stanley Johnston watched the *Lexington* gunners go into action: "There is the sharp 'wham-wham-wham-wham-wham' of the 5 inchers, the staccato bark of the 1.1 inchers, and the rushing yammer of the 20mm batteries. A hellish chorus, uneven, jerky, but so forceful that it leaves us, there on the bridge, gasping in the partial vacuums created by the blasts. . . . Our nostrils are stung by the reeking cordite of the driving charges. Up from the port side of the ship goes a curtain of tracer, winking red and white in the brilliant sunshine. . ."

In a perfectly coordinated attack, Kate torpedo bombers came in on the *Lexington* from both sides to drop their deadly fish. At one point, eleven torpedo wakes were counted heading toward the "Lady Lex." Captain Frederick C. Sherman maneuvered the big ship desperately, but two torpedoes crashed into her port side. At the same time, Val dive bombers scored two hits and several near misses alongside that damaged the hull. In the midst of the attack, the ship's siren was set off by a bomb fragment and added its shriek to the din of battle.

The *Yorktown,* too, came under attack, but she was a smaller and more maneuverable ship and avoided all the torpedoes launched at her. One bomb went through the flight deck, causing extensive damage deep in the hull and killing or wounding sixty-nine men, but she was still able to handle her planes.

By noon, the Battle of the Coral Sea was over. The Japanese invasion fleet bound for Port Moresby turned back.

The *Shoho* had been lost, and Hara's task force was crippled, with one carrier badly damaged and only thirty-nine planes left of an original complement of 125. One more act remained, however, before the final curtain fell.

The crew of the battered *Lexington* worked fast and skillfully, and before long she was steaming at twenty-five knots and taking planes aboard. The damage control officer reported to Captain Sherman, "We've got the torpedo damage temporarily shored up, the fires out, and soon will have the ship back on an even keel. But I would suggest, sir, that if you have to take any more torpedoes, you take 'em on the starboard side."

Yet the Lady Lex's luck was running out. A generator was left on near a damaged tank of aviation gasoline, and an hour after the attack, a spark from the motor ignited gasoline fumes. A tremendous explosion shook the ship from stem to stern. Other explosions followed. The crew redoubled its efforts, but in midafternoon, a second great explosion rocked the carrier, and fires blazed out of control. Captain Sherman ordered the crew to abandon ship.

Every compartment that could be reached was checked to see that no one was left aboard. Sailors finished off the ship's supply of ice cream before going over the side, and even the captain's dog was saved. Sherman was the last to leave, sliding down a rope from the flight deck into the warm sea. Every man who abandoned ship was rescued by the escort vessels.

The *Lexington* was soon torn by almost continuous explosions. "In the deepening twilight it was a sight of awful majesty," wrote correspondent Stanley Johnston. "The leaping, towering flames . . . hid all feebler light from the skies. Every bit of flotsam and every outline of the great ship showed up in a blinding glare."

Admiral Fletcher sadly ordered a destroyer to torpedo the blazing hulk so it would not be a beacon to guide the Japanese to the task force. Three torpedoes struck home, and at 8:00 p.m., the Lady Lex slid under. "There she goes," said one of her officers. "She didn't turn over. She's going down with her head up . . . a lady to the last!"

With that, the curtain dropped on the drama of

the Coral Sea. The opposing ships steamed away to nurse their wounds and prepare for other battles. They had never once sighted each other. For the first time in history, a naval battle had been fought entirely by carrier aircraft.

3
DECISION AT MIDWAY

Although Admiral Isoroku Yamamoto, commander in chief of the Imperial Japanese Navy, believed in taking major risks to achieve victory, he also believed in being totally realistic. He was convinced that his navy must crush the U.S. Pacific Fleet at the earliest possible moment in 1942, before America's industrial power began to make its weight felt in the Pacific war.

Yamamoto had long supported naval air power. As early as 1915, when asked about the navy of the future, he had replied: "The most important ship of the future will be a ship to carry airplanes." He pushed Japan's carrier development hard in the 1930s, and in 1941 masterminded the strike at

Pearl Harbor. American naval officers who had known Yamamoto before the war respected him as a tough and canny foe.

The Japanese had achieved so much so quickly in the first months of war that they were not quite sure what to do next. Some of the warlords favored an advance eastward against India and Ceylon. Others wanted to cut Australia's links to the United States by seizing the New Hebrides, Fiji, and Samoa islands. Admiral Yamamoto, however, opposed all such moves without first removing the U.S. Navy from the board. The best way to do this, he said, was a thrust against the Hawaiian Islands to force Admiral Nimitz into battle.

It was the Doolittle-Halsey raid on April 18, 1942, that settled the argument. The B-25s did more damage to Japanese pride than to Japanese cities; Yamamoto particularly "lost face," and renewed his demands to go after Nimitz's carriers. This time there was no debate. Yamamoto set early June as a target date for the decisive battle.

The Imperial Navy considered the Coral Sea fight a good omen, claiming one American fleet carrier sunk and a second one, the *Yorktown* - probably sunk. Even though the light carrier *Shoho* was lost and the fleet carriers *Shokaku* and *Zuikaku* were scratched from the coming operation - the one because of battle damage, the other because of the need to train new aircrews to replace those lost - Yamamoto remained confident.

The Japanese admiral did not intend to miss his chance through caution or weakness. Under his prodding was assembled the most powerful fleet the world had ever seen: eight aircraft carriers, eleven battleships, twenty-two cruisers, sixty-seven destroyers, twenty-one submarines, and scores of transports, tankers, and smaller craft. Aboard the carriers were 411 fighters and bombers. The commander in chief himself would sail in the super-battleship *Yamato*.

This enormous fleet was divided into four major striking forces. A two-carrier task force would raid the Aleutian Islands, which stretch westward from Alaska, hoping to decoy Nimitz into moving north. The other three forces were to be thrown against Midway, the westernmost military outpost of the Hawaiian Islands, some 1,100 miles from Pearl Harbor.

Admiral Chuichi Nagumo, commander of the Pearl Harbor attack, would lead the Carrier Striking Force *(Akagi, Kaga, Hiryu,* and *Soryu)* in softening up Midway for invasion. The Occupation Force, consisting of transports covered by a light carrier and two battleships, would make the landing. Lurking in the background would be Yamamoto's Main Body, including seven battleships and a light carrier, ready to join Nagumo's carriers in the kill if Nimitz came out to fight. With Midway in his hands and the U.S. Pacific Fleet at the bottom of the ocean, Yamamoto could think at his leisure about taking Pearl Harbor.

One of the cardinal rules of war is concentration of forces at the point of attack. By dividing his strength, Yamamoto appeared to be violating this rule, yet he felt his reasoning was sound. He expected that the Midway assault would come as a surprise to the Americans and that he would have plenty of time to pull together his total strength to meet any counter-stroke. In addition, there was a chance that Nimitz might take the Aleutians' bait and be trapped between converging forces. Finally, whichever way Nimitz jumped, Japanese submarines stationed off Hawaii would signal the moment any U.S. naval forces left Pearl Harbor.

There was one further point Yamamoto considered in his favor - confidence in victory. In nearly six months of fighting, the biggest warships the Imperial Navy had lost were two destroyers and one light carrier. His planes were proven, and his men battle-tested. In boxing terms, Uncle Sam had taken a bad beating in round one, and in round two, Yamamoto was setting himself to throw the knockout punch.

Unknown to the Japanese commander in chief, he lost the advantage of surprise even before his ships left their bases in late May. With persistence and skill, Naval Intelligence not only analyzed Japanese radio traffic but even managed to crack some of Yamamoto's naval codes. As a result, Intelligence worked out the size and makeup of the various enemy forces and decided that something very big was about to happen in the Hawaiian area.

Japanese radio traffic referred to the target simply as "AF." Admiral King in Washington thought AF was Pearl Harbor; Admiral Nimitz was equally sure it was Midway. To settle the matter, Intelligence told Midway to send an uncoded radio message complaining that its distillation plant for converting salt water to fresh water had broken down. The Japanese obligingly rose to the lure, and soon a message was intercepted reporting AF to be low on water.

Despite the evidence furnished by Intelligence, Admiral Nimitz had a difficult decision to make. A number of his staff officers thought the whole Intelligence breakthrough was nothing more than an elaborate Japanese ruse to fool the Americans into pulling their fleet back to the Hawaiian Islands. According to this theory, the Imperial Navy could then resume without opposition its South Pacific offensive that had been interrupted by the Coral Sea battle. Nimitz, however, decided to take this risk. Ignoring the Australian lifeline as well as the feint at the Aleutians, he concentrated on the defense of Midway.

Analyzing Japanese intentions, however, was only one of his problems. The *Lexington* was at the bottom of the Coral Sea, and the *Yorktown* had taken a serious hit in that action. The *Saratoga* was on the West Coast, still training a new air group. The *Enterprise* and the *Hornet*, which had rushed southward toward the Coral Sea, were ordered back to Pearl Harbor on the double. They arrived on May 26, and the next afternoon, the battered *Yorktown* steamed up the channel and into dry dock. It was estimated that the damage caused by the Japanese bomb would take weeks to repair. Admiral Nimitz disagreed.

Some 1,400 workmen swarmed aboard the *Yorktown*. They patched leaks caused by near-misses and tore out crumpled deck plates and bulkheads deep in the hull. New ones were made and welded into place, electric cables and steam lines were replaced, and equipment of every kind was repaired. The work continued without pause, and on May 29, only two days after her arrival, the *Yorktown* moved out of dry dock to take on fuel and new planes.

The *Yorktown* and her escorts, two cruisers and five destroyers, made up Admiral Frank Jack Fletcher's Task Force 17. Waiting 350 miles northeast of Midway was Task Force 16 - the carriers *Hornet* and *Enterprise*, six cruisers, and nine destroyers under Rear Admiral Raymond A. Spruance. He had replaced Admiral Halsey, who was hospitalized with a skin disease. Although this was his first carrier command, Spruance had a cool competence that meshed well with Halsey's experienced staff.

In the late afternoon of June 2, Task Forces 16 and 17 joined to await the enemy. Fletcher was the senior officer and assumed command. He and Spruance, with but twenty-five ships and 233 carrier planes to pit against Yamamoto's huge force, staked everything on achieving surprise. They planned to tie well to the north of Midway and rely on search planes from the island to spot the Japanese. Then they would move in fast and launch a heavy air strike at Yamamoto's carriers. The carriers were the key; without the air cover they provided, the rest of the Japanese fleet would be wide open to attack from the sky.

By setting up his ambush well in advance, Nimitz sabotaged another important part of Yamamoto's plan. The submarines the Japanese admiral counted on to shadow the American fleet arrived at their stations between Midway and Pearl Harbor on June 3 - much too late to sight Task Forces 16 and 17 slipping away to the north.

At dawn on June 3, 1942, the stage was set for the Battle of Midway. Far to the north the carriers *Ryujo* and *Junyo* readied a strike at American bases in the Aleutians. The Japanese Occupation Force was some 700 miles due west of Midway. Angling in from the northwest, and slightly farther from Midway, was Admiral Nagumo's

Carrier Striking Force; about 300 miles astern of Nagumo were the heavy guns of Yamamoto's Main Body. Unknown to the enemy, the three U.S. carriers were circling patiently northeast of Midway. As one historian of the battle put it, "the hunter had become the hunted."

June 3 was a day of tension and alarms. At dawn, Japanese planes bombed the Aleutians, paving the way for troops to land on two small islands, Attu and Kiska, at the very tip of the Aleutian chain. In mid-morning, a Catalina flying boat from Midway spotted a group of ships west of the island. Fletcher correctly decided this must be the Occupation Force, which he knew would mark time until American opposition had been eliminated. He saved his precious advantage of surprise for bigger game. That night, Catalinas attempted a moonlight torpedo attack on the Occupation Force, damaging one tanker.

Nagumo's four carriers rushed at twenty-five knots through the darkness toward Midway. Fletcher and Spruance were also on the move that night, aiming for a dawn position that would put them within striking distance of the enemy carriers. June 4 was clearly going to be the day of battle, and a good deal would depend on which side made the first sighting.

In the faint light of dawn on June 4, eleven long-range Catalinas climbed slowly from Midway and headed west to search. At the same time, Nagumo's crews swung into action, preparing fighters and bombers for the softening-up strike at Midway. At 4:30 a.m., the launching signal was given. Thirty-six Zeros bounded off the flight decks, followed by thirty-six Val dive bombers and thirty-six heavily loaded Kates. Lieutenant Joichi Tomonaga led the strike force toward Midway, 240 miles to the east. Admiral Nagumo also ordered his escort ships to catapult a scouting force of seven seaplanes for a precautionary search to the north.

Aboard the three U.S. carrier, hundreds of tense airmen waited in their ready rooms. Twice they were ordered to man their planes, only to be called back. Teletype machines that flashed flight data on screens in the ready rooms were silent, and one pilot recalled glaring almost resentfully at the telephone "talker" who sat maddeningly still, listening for orders from the bridge.

At 5:45 a.m., one of the Catalina pilots radioed: "Many enemy planes heading Midway." Fifteen minutes later, Fletcher and Spruance got the message they had been waiting for. A second Catalina reported the position, course, and speed of the Japanese carrier force. Fletcher signaled Spruance's Task Force 16 to head toward the enemy at top speed. He would follow with the *Yorktown* as soon as he recovered his dawn patrol of scout planes. Spruance estimated that in an hour, the

Enterprise and the *Hornet* would reach a position within range of the enemy carriers.

At Midway, every plane that could fly was sent into the air, the bombers to go after the Japanese carriers, and the fighters to intercept the incoming strike force. The island's Marine fighter squadron consisted of six Wildcats and twenty old Brewster Buffalos, cast-off carrier fighters that were sadly out of date. Lieutenant Tomonaga's Zeros dove on the Marine fighters and shot down fifteen of them. The Vals and Kates hit Midway hard, smashing hangars and oil tanks and the powerhouse but failing to wreck the airfield. Heading back to the carriers, Tomonaga radioed Admiral Nagumo that Midway's airfield would need a second raid.

Nagumo's hands were full just then. Four Army B-26 bombers and six Navy Grumman Avengers from Midway were making a desperate attempt to aim torpedoes at the Japanese carriers. Hounded by patrolling Zeros, none of them scored any hits, and all but three were shot down. Nevertheless, the Japanese admiral began to feel decidedly uneasy. As one of his officers later wrote, "Somehow we resembled a man walking through a lonely forest with a bag of gold on his shoulder, an inviting prey for the first robber who saw the chance to pounce upon him."

Nagumo had held back half his planes in case American ships were sighted, but no word had come in from his scouting seaplanes, and the attack just beaten off confirmed that Midway did, indeed, need a second raid. After pacing the *Akagi's* bridge for fifteen minutes, Nagumo made his decision. At 7:15, he ordered the Kates on the flight decks of the *Akagi* and the *Kaga* to be sent below to have their torpedoes replaced by heavy bombs more suited to targets on Midway.

At that moment, some 200 miles away, Admiral Spruance too had to make an agonizing decision. If he launched immediately, he stood a chance of catching the enemy carriers when they were most vulnerable - refueling and rearming the planes returned from the Midway strike. But he also had to face the hard fact that many of his planes might not have enough fuel to make it back to their carriers. After pondering a moment, Spruance decided to take the risk and hit with everything he had; he ordered off all the attack planes that could fly.

While Nagumo's crewmen worked furiously at the backbreaking job of rearming the Kates with bombs, a series of very disturbing messages began to come in from one of the scouting seaplanes launched earlier by the Japanese cruiser *Tone.* Its pilot first reported vaguely that he had sighted to the north "what appears to be ten enemy surface ships." While waiting impatiently for more information, Nagumo ordered work on the torpedo bombers to stop. It was now eight o'clock, and once more the Japanese admiral was distracted by American attackers from Midway.

Sixteen Dauntlesses flown by inexperienced Marine pilots glided in to attack the Japanese carriers and were shot to ribbons by Zeros and antiaircraft fire. A few moments later, huge geysers of water erupted around the carriers as Army Flying Fortress bombers tried to hit the twisting ships from almost four miles up. Like the Marine Dauntlesses, they scored no hits, nor did a third attack a few minutes later by another squadron of Marine bombers. These obsolete Vought Vindicators - which their disgusted Marine pilots called Vibrators - made a fruitless attack on a Japanese battleship.

As the surviving American planes disappeared in the distance, Admiral Nagumo faced a second critical decision. The *Tone*'s search plane had finally reported that "the enemy is accompanied by what appears to be a carrier." Just as Nagumo ordered the Kates to be armed once again with torpedoes so they could attack ships, his Midway strike force returned.

Nagumo could either immediately launch those bombers of the reserve force still on the flight decks, without fighter escorts, against the carrier that the search plane had sighted or he could send them below, recover the Midway raiders, and later send off a strong, well-balanced force to hit the enemy. He chose the second course.

The returning planes began landing shortly after 8:30 and crewmen set to work at a frantic pace. The flight decks had to be cleared, the returning planes refueled and rearmed, and a new strike force "re-spotted" for takeoff. When the last plane was aboard, Admiral Nagumo turned away from Midway and began steaming at top speed toward the point where the U.S. ships had been sighted.

Nagumo began to feel somewhat easier. Midway had been heavily damaged, every enemy attack had been beaten off, and the Americans apparently had but one carrier to oppose his four. He hoped the change of course would throw off any more assaults for the hour that he needed to prepare his air strike.

At the time that Admiral Nagumo made his course change, 151 U.S. carrier planes were winging across the Pacific. Admiral Spruance had virtually emptied the *Hornet* and the *Enterprise*, keeping back only enough fighters for a combat air patrol over Task Force 16. Admiral Fletcher also held back a fighter patrol, as well as half his dive bombers in case of emergency.

According to the training books, ideal attack strategy called for a simultaneous strike by torpedo bombers and dive bombers, with covering fighters driving off enemy interceptors. On this day, however, the Americans had to ignore the rules in order to have enough gasoline to return. The heavily loaded Devastator torpedo bombers, for example, stayed low and set right out for the enemy, saving both the time and the gas required to climb and join their fighter escorts. Then the weather caused further confusion: The torpedo bombers were low, the fighters and dive bombers high, and with clouds in between, visual contact was lost. Finally, due to Nagumo's change of course, the Americans peered down at a vast expanse of empty ocean at the point where the Japanese carriers were supposed to be.

The commander of the *Hornet*'s fighters and dive bombers guessed the Japanese had continued on toward Midway at increased speed, turned in that direction, and so took forty-five planes out of the battle. The other squadron leaders, however, suspected what had happened and searched in the other direction. Before long they were rewarded by the sight of white, featherlike ships' wakes in the distance.

The first to sight the Japanese carriers was Lieutenant Commander John Waldron's Torpedo 8 squadron from the *Hornet*, flying without fighter cover. Eight miles short of their targets, the fifteen Devastators were pounced on by Zeros. One after another the lumbering TBDs were torn apart or set ablaze. Miles away, a dive bomber pilot heard Waldron say over the radio, "Attack immediately. There are two fighters in the water. . .My two wingmen are going in the water. . .," then silence.

Every one of Torpedo 8's planes was shot down, and only one man, Ensign George Gay, survived. Gay crawled out of his sinking plane, inflated his life jacket, and hid under a seat cushion to watch the battle from a ringside seat.

Waldron's attack had been made at 9:30 a.m. A few minutes later, the *Enterprise* torpedo squadron bored in to attack. The Zeros swarmed in for the kill and shot down ten of the fourteen Devastators. At 10:00, it was the turn of the *Yorktown* TBDs. Ten of them also went cartwheeling into the sea. Of the forty-one Devastators, thirty-five had been lost, and not a single one of their torpedoes had found its mark.

Throughout the attack, the sweating Japanese crews were preparing planes for launching. At 10:20, *Akagi, Kaga, Soryu,* and *Hiryu* turned into the wind, and Admiral Nagumo gave the long-awaited order to launch planes.

Just then, some 15,000 feet up, pilots and gunners in fifty-four Dauntless dive bombers were staring in amazement at the sight below. "I had an intoxicating view of the whole Japanese fleet," said *Enterprise* pilot Clarence Dickinson. "This was the culmination of our hopes and dreams. Among those ships I could see two long, narrow, yellow rectangles, the flight decks of carriers . . . that yellow stood out on the dark blue sea like nothing you have ever seen. Then farther off I saw a third carrier . . . The southwest corner of the fleet's position was obscured by a storm area. Suddenly another long yellow rectangle came sliding out of that obscurity. A fourth carrier!

"I could not understand why we had come this far without having fighters swarming over and around us like hornets. But we hadn't seen a single fighter in the air and not a shot had been fired at us."

The reason that Lieutenant Dickinson saw no fighters was that every Zero of the combat air patrol had streaked down to low altitude to slaughter the torpedo bombers. Too late, the Zero pilots saw the high-flying Dauntlesses; too late they put their fighters into maximum climbs.

The American squadron leaders calmly picked their targets. The *Yorktown's* Lieutenant Commander Maxwell Leslie chose the *Kaga* for his seventeen SBDs. Lieutenant Commander Clarence McClusky divided the *Enterprise's* thirty-seven dive bombers between the *Akagi* and the *Soryu*. The *Hiryu* was several miles distant, and there was no time to reach her. As they rolled over into their dives, the American pilots could see Zeros racing off the crowded flight decks below. The first warning the Japanese crewmen had was a rising screech of diving planes heard over the noise of their own planes warming up for takeoff.

"The target was utterly satisfying," said Lieutenant

Dickinson. "The squadron's dive was perfect. This was the absolute. After this, I felt, anything would be just anticlimax. I saw the bombs from the group commander's section drop. They struck the water on either side of the *[Akagi]* . . . I had picked as my point of aim the big red disk with its band of white up on the bow. Near the dropping point I saw a bomb hit just behind where I was aiming . . . I saw the deck rippling and curling back in all directions, exposing a great section of the hangar below . . .

"I had determined during that dive that since I was dropping on a Japanese carrier I was going to see my bomb hit. After dropping I kicked my rudder to get my tail out of the way and put my plane in a stall. So I was simply standing there to watch it. I saw the 500-pound bomb hit right abreast of the island . . ."

Torpedoes in the Kates - the torpedoes the Japanese crewmen had been manhandling for three hours - blew up with a roar. One of the *Akagi's* officers saw the wrecked planes on the flight deck "tail up, belching livid flame and jet-black smoke." Another officer remembered a "terrific fire aboard ship which was just like hell." As the fires spread out of control, the ammunition in antiaircraft guns began to go off. The order to abandon ship was given, and crewmen dived overboard to escape the blistering heat and the repeated explosions. Admiral Nagumo at first refused to leave his flagship and had to be dragged off the bridge.

The rest of the *Enterprise* SBDs plummeted down on the *Soryu*. In rapid succession, three 1,000-pound bombs scored. One went through the deck and exploded in the hangar, blowing the forward elevator upward and back against the island (the superstructure on the edge of the flight deck). The other two bombs struck among the parked planes on the deck, setting off raging gasoline fires and flinging into the sea a Zero that was just taking off.

The *Soryu's*, engines died, and she wallowed to a stop, burning like a Roman candle. The crew abandoned ship, but her captain refused to leave. He was last seen standing erect on the bridge, clouds of black smoke boiling around him.

Commander Leslie led the *Yorktown* Dauntlesses against the *Kaga*. Like the *Enterprise* bombers, they met no Zeros and only light antiaircraft fire. Leslie's release mechanism had gone awry during the flight, dropping his bomb harmlessly into the ocean, and all he could do was spray the carrier with machine-gun bullets as he dived. But his men planted four 1,000-pound bombs on the Kaga, one wrecking the island, the others splintering the flight deck and bursting a fuel storage tank. Flaming rivers of gasoline from the tank and from wrecked planes coursed down into the hull, setting off stored bombs that blew the ship apart.

The entire spectacular attack lasted just two minutes. By 10:30 a.m., ten minutes after Admiral Nagumo had given the order to launch planes, three of his carriers were mortally wounded.

An American pilot radioed Spruance and Fletcher, "They're all afire. But I can't tell you what ships they are. You can make out the typical Dutch-shoe bows but they're all afire amidships and the smoke is rolling back so you can't even see how long they are."

The frustrated Zero pilots finally got into the fight as the Dauntlesses pulled out of their dives and went scurrying away just above the wave tops. Although they knocked down several bombers, they in turn took a beating from the SBD rear gunners. As soon as the American pilots eluded their pursuers, they throttled back to save gas for the long trip back to the carriers. It was a close call for many of them; Commander McClusky, for example, landed on the *Enterprise* with only two gallons of gas left. Others ditched their planes near escort vessels and were rescued. All told, the attack cost 16 sixteen Dauntlesses.

Despite the disaster that had overtaken him, Admiral Nagumo ordered his one remaining carrier, the *Hiryu,* to continue the fight. At noon, eighteen Val dive bombers escorted by six fighters were sighted on the *Yorktown*'s radar. Six of the Vals fought their way through the protecting screen of Wildcats to score three hits on the carrier. One bomb set several planes on the hangar deck ablaze, a second started a fire near the forward gasoline storage tanks, and the third tore into the smokestack, knocking out the power plant. Damage control parties went to work quickly, and in less than two hours, they had the fires under control and steam up.

Then a second wave of *Hiryu* planes plunged in, and two torpedoes ripped into the carrier's hull. The boiler rooms flooded, and the *Yorktown* again lost power and came to a stop, this time taking on a dangerous list. Fearing she was about to capsize, the captain gave the abandon ship order.

Within two hours, the *Yorktown* was avenged. A strike force from the *Enterprise,* including ten orphaned *Yorktown* planes, caught the *Hiryu* preparing to launch her remaining bombers. Once more the SBDs screamed down out of the sky, and once more the effect was lethal. Four heavy bombs slashed into the vulnerable carrier, blowing the forward elevator completely out of the flight deck, splashing blazing gasoline everywhere, and turning the ship into a funeral pyre for hundreds of men.

One by one, during the night and into the next day, the four carriers of the once-proud Carrier Striking Force disappeared into the depths. Shortly after 7:00 p.m., a last great explosion of her magazines tore the *Soryu* in two. A few minutes later, the blazing

Kaga blew up and sank. The gutted *Akagi* was put out of her agony at dawn on June 5 by torpedoes from a Japanese destroyer, and a few hours, later the *Hiryu* joined her.

News of the destruction of the Carrier Striking Force struck Admiral Yamamoto like a body blow, leaving him "too stunned to speak." But he rallied quickly, ordering his scattered forces to concentrate, trying to salvage victory from defeat by luring his opponent under the great guns of the Japanese battleships. Admiral Spruance, who took over command when Fletcher abandoned the crippled *Yorktown*, had no intention of throwing away the hard-won triumph. For two days, the fleets advanced and retreated, Spruance always staying out of reach of the enemy's guns. On June 6, his planes struck the final blow by sinking the heavy cruiser *Mikuma*.

Finally, Admiral Yamamoto admitted defeat and ordered his ships to retire eastward. Never in modern history had Japan suffered such a crushing defeat. Yamamoto had lost four fleet carriers, a cruiser, nearly 300 planes, and some 3,500 men.

Had it not been for the Japanese submarine I-168, American losses at Midway would have stood at 140 planes. On June 6, the sturdy *Yorktown* was still afloat and being towed slowly toward Pearl Harbor. The destroyer *Hammann* was tied up alongside, providing power for a repair crew. In the early afternoon, *I-168* crept under the ring of patrolling destroyers and fired four torpedoes. One missed, two ripped into the carrier, and the fourth broke the back of the *Hammann*. The destroyer went down immediately, but the *Yorktown* lingered on through the night.

"At dawn it was evident she was doomed," wrote historian Samuel Eliot Morison. "The escorting destroyers half-masted their colors, all hands came to attention, uncovered; and at 0600, with her loose gear making a horrible death rattle, *Yorktown* rolled over and sank in a 2,000-fathom deep."

So ended the Battle of Midway.

4
TAKING THE OFFENSIVE

The Battle of Midway had been won, and won brilliantly, by U.S. carrier forces, and historians rank it as a major turning point of World War II. While those who planned and fought the battle sensed its historic importance, its most immediate result was a welcome relief from Japanese pressure, a breathing space in which to take stock and to prepare for further battles.

In spite of the victory, the outlook in the Pacific remained dark in that summer of 1942. Japan's ocean empire spanned the South Pacific from the Philippines and the Netherlands East Indies to New Guinea, the Bismarck Archipelago, and the Solomon Islands. Guarding the Central Pacific were four large Japanese-held island groups: the

Marianas, the Carolines, the Marshalls, and the Gilberts. Far to the north, the Japanese clung to footholds on Kiska and Attu in the Aleutians. From the twin centers of Truk in the Carolines and Rabaul in the Bismarcks radiated a spider's web of defenses that included thousands of ships and planes and hundreds of thousands of troops.

The Allied line formed a great arc beyond the fringes of this empire, anchored on the north by the Hawaiian Islands and on the south by Australia and New Zealand. These bastions were linked by a chain of island bases, the most important being Samoa, Fiji, New Caledonia, and the New Hebrides. With war production at home running far behind demand, commanders manning this line were told they could expect a mere handful of Army and Marine divisions and only a few new ships - none of them fleet carriers - for the rest of the year and well into 1943.

Admiral King, however, was outspoken about the need to start an offensive in the Pacific without delay and regardless of the difficulties. As early as March, 1942, three months before Midway, the aggressive commander of the fleet proposed to President Roosevelt that a thrust be made into the Solomon Islands. This, said King, should be step one in a march on the Japanese fortress of Rabaul in the Bismarcks. In May, he became more insistent when the enemy seized Tulagi in the southern Solomons. By July, King had won his point completely. The Japanese were spotted building an airfield on Guadalcanal Island, a few miles from Tulagi; unless a fast counterstroke was made in the Solomons, they would soon be in excellent position to threaten the American lifeline to Australia.

Operation Watchtower - the invasion of Guadalcanal - was scheduled for early August. The First Marine Division was to land and seize the airfield, under air cover from Admiral Fletcher's carriers. Fletcher picked *Saratoga, Enterprise,* and *Wasp* (newly arrived from duty in the Atlantic) for the job, holding the *Hornet* in reserve.

On August 7, 1942, eight months to the day after Pearl Harbor, the United States took the offensive against Japan. The Marines rushed ashore on Guadalcanal, scattered the surprised defenders, and captured the airstrip. Named Henderson Field for a Marine dive bomber pilot killed at Midway, it soon became the focus of the most savage kind of combat. No other World War II battle was fought over so small a piece of ground for so long at so high a cost.

The little escort carrier *Long Island,* a one-time cattle boat with a flight deck atop her hull, delivered thirty-one very welcome Wildcats and Dauntlesses to the Henderson Field Marines on August 20. The same day, Admiral Yamamoto set in motion a counterattack. Out of Truk harbor steamed a powerful fleet that included three carriers and three battleships.

On August 23, a series of false alarms sent American carrier planes searching in vain for the enemy ships. That evening, Fletcher decided the Japanese were not close enough to cause any trouble and sent the *Wasp* off to refuel. This left only the *Saratoga* and the *Enterprise,* the battleship *North Carolina*, and a screen of cruisers and destroyers to face the onrushing enemy. Vice Admiral Chuichi Nagumo, victor at Pearl Harbor and loser at Midway, commanded the main striking force built around the big carriers *Shokaku* and *Zuikaku,* both veterans of the Coral Sea battle. Ranging out ahead was a "bait force" centered on the light carrier *Ryujo,* led by Fletcher's Coral Sea opponent, Rear Admiral Tadaichi Hara. On the morning of August 24, Hara's ships were sighted by American planes, and the Battle of the Eastern Solomons was on.

As the wily Yamamoto had hoped, Fletcher sent most of his planes after Hara's bait force. It was late afternoon when the *Saratoga's* dive bomber squadron found the *Ryujo.* These bomber pilots had served aboard the *Yorktown* at Midway - the *Saratoga* was then out of action - and they knew just what to do when an enemy carrier came into sight below. The SBDs rolled over from 14,000 feet and splattered the little *Ryujo* with 1,000-pound bombs.

A few minutes later, one of the new Grumman TBF Avengers, the much-needed replacements for the old Devastators, put a torpedo into the burning carrier. She took on a severe list, and her engines stopped; four hours later she turned over and sank.

Fletcher's carriers had not escaped the prying eyes of enemy scout planes; even as the bait carrier took her fatal beating, fighters and bombers were racing off the decks of the *Shokaku* and the *Zuikaku*. Here was the chance Admiral Nagumo had been waiting for since his humiliation at Midway.

Radar warned of the Japanese air strike when it was still ninety miles from the American fleet. The *Saratoga* and the *Enterprise* were ten miles apart, each ringed closely by escorts. More than fifty Wildcats formed a combat air patrol. The ships' crews waited tensely at battle stations - all guns manned, all watertight compartment doors shut, all damage control parties alerted.

The Wildcats raced to the attack, and escorting Zeros met them head on to keep them away from the bombers. The Japanese fighter pilots did their job well, and few Wildcats got through the defensive screen; those that did, however, scored heavily.

Pilot Donald Runyon of the *Enterprise*'s "Grim Reapers" fighter squadron dived out of the sun at an unwary Val dive bomber and blew it to pieces. Repeating the tactic of attacking with the sun behind him, he turned a second Val into a flaming torch. (Japanese fighters and bombers, unlike U.S. planes, had little protective armor; they also lacked self-sealing gas tanks with special linings that closed up bullet holes to prevent fires and explosions.) Runyon then maneuvered out of the way of a Zero that was sitting on his tail; as the Japanese fighter sped by underneath, he nosed the F4F down, pressed the firing button, and ripped the Zero apart. Zooming upward again, Runyon put a long burst of machine-gun fire into the underside of yet another Val, setting it afire. He closed out his shooting exhibition by damaging a Zero that belatedly tried to interfere.

The heroics of Runyon and his fellow Wildcat pilots hurt but did not stop Nagumo's strike force. Failing to sight the *Saratoga*, the attackers concentrated their entire strength on the *Enterprise.*

A string of thirty Vals peeled off and dived down on the twisting American carrier. A 1,000-pounder with a delayed fuze ripped through the after elevator and two decks before exploding. A half-minute later, a second bomb hit in nearly the same spot, wiping out thirty-nine men in the gun gallery just below the edge of the flight deck. Ninety seconds later, a third bomb blew a hole in the flight deck near the island.

The first hit was the most serious, starting fires and tearing gashes in the hull that let in the sea.

Damage control parties rigged water hoses and repaired electrical circuits to provide light for the firefighters. Crewmen rushed into the flaming gun gallery to throw ammunition overboard before it blew up. Gradually, the fires were beaten back, and the holes in the hull patched with mattresses and timbers. Steel plates were spiked over the shattered flight deck planking. Less than an hour after the attack, the Big E was apparently out of danger and taking aboard her planes.

Deep in the hull, however, just forward of the rudder, the crew of the steering control room was in trouble. The first bomb had exploded close above the compartment, and smoke poured in on the men through the ventilating system. When they shut off the vent, the temperature climbed steadily until it reached 160 degrees. Finally, when neither men nor machinery could take the heat any longer, the ventilator was reopened. Water, fumes, and fire-fighting chemicals flooded into the compartment, short-circuiting the steering motor that moved the huge rudder and knocking out the crewmen before they could switch over to the standby motor.

The Big E's rudder jammed, and at twenty-four knots, she heeled over in an out-of-control turn, warning sirens shrieking. The captain of the destroyer *Balch* saw 20,000 tons of aircraft carrier bearing down on him, called for full speed ahead, and skipped out of the way safely. As the *Enterprise* slowed to ten knots and circled helplessly, the radar room reported an enemy strike force fifteen minutes' flying time away.

Chief Machinist Mate William Smith guessed immediately what had happened in the steering control room. Putting on an oxygen mask and stuffing tools into his pockets, Smith tried to reach the compartment through the wrecked after section of the ship. Twice he was driven back by still-burning debris. The third time, he fought his way into the control room and switched over to the standby motor. All but one of the steering crew survived. In the meantime, relieved radarmen watched the blips fade from their screens as the Japanese planes turned the wrong way. The Big E's crew never again had a doubt that she was a good-luck ship.

The Battle of the Eastern Solomons was another defeat for Admiral Nagumo. The Americans considered the damage to the *Enterprise* and the loss of seventeen planes more than offset by the destruction of the *Ryujo* and seventy Japanese planes. Yet the fleet carriers *Shokaku* and *Zuikaku* remained intact, and their presence was made more and more ominous by the events of the next three weeks.

On August 31, a Japanese submarine put a torpedo into the *Saratoga* - her second of the war - and old

"Sara" joined the *Enterprise* on the sidelines for repairs. Now only two U.S. fleet carriers, the *Wasp* and the *Hornet,* were operational in the Pacific, and they were tethered to Guadalcanal to counter any move by the Imperial Navy. The Japanese knew this fact as well as anyone, and on the afternoon of September 15, exactly what American carrier men had been dreading took place.

The *Wasp* and the *Hornet* were patrolling in the Coral Sea south of Guadalcanal that afternoon when they ran into an undersea ambush. A Japanese submarine slammed three torpedoes into the *Wasp's* starboard side. The explosions sent tremendous jolts lashing through the ship, shattering machinery, tumbling planes, and breaking water mains used for fire-fighting. Flames burst out on the hangar deck where planes were being refueled, and a huge column of smoke boiled upward. Minutes later a second sub fired a spread of torpedoes at the *Hornet.* The Japanese skipper's aim was a bit off, and he missed the carrier, but one torpedo tore an eighteen by thirty-two-foot gash in the hull of the battleship *North Carolina* and another ripped open the destroyer *O'Brien.*

"*Wasp* in the meantime was being eaten alive by fire," wrote historian Samuel Eliot Morison. "Faster and faster the swirling yellow flames moved, taller and taller they flared." The wrecked water system made fire-fighting nearly impossible, and one explosion followed another as the flames reached fuel tanks and bomb magazines. The abandon ship order was given, and a destroyer sank the burning derelict. The *Wasp*, which had fought gallantly in the Atlantic and in the Mediterranean, went down before having a chance to take part in a Pacific battle. Her loss left Admiral Nimitz with only one carrier in fighting trim.

The situation on Guadalcanal was becoming as grave as the situation at sea. At night, the Japanese kept slipping fresh troops ashore from fast transports and destroyers with such regularity that the Americans began calling this supply line the "Tokyo Express." The Marines threw back every assault, but warfare in the steaming, stinking jungle was taking a heavy toll of men and machines. At Henderson Field, no matter what the type of plane or where it came from, wrote Morison, "if it had wings it flew; if it flew it fought; and if it fought very long, something was certain to happen to it."

At first, the Japanese tried to recapture Guadalcanal and advance in New Guinea at the same time, with the result that both offensives were shorthanded. In September, the warlords ordered the New Guinea operation to a halt and concentrated on Guadalcanal. The Tokyo Express stepped up its pace. Cruisers and destroyers bombarded the Marine defenses almost nightly. One night in mid-October, a pair of Japanese battleships plastered

Henderson Field with some 900 huge shells. "But it wasn't that," said one of the demoralized men at the airfield. "It was the hopelessness, the feeling that nobody gave a curse whether we lived or died."

Then, on October 18, Admiral Nimitz placed tough, aggressive Bill Halsey in charge of the campaign. Six days later, President Roosevelt, putting aside the pressing needs of the European theater, ordered reinforcements to the South Pacific. With a new hand at the helm, backed by the highest authority in the nation, the United States was now completely committed to holding Guadalcanal.

Hardly had Halsey taken command when the Japanese struck once more. Admiral Yamamoto ordered an attack by his fleet against the U.S. naval forces that was timed to match a ground assault on Henderson Field. While Admiral Nagumo's strengthened task force - the fleet carriers *Shokaku, Zuikaku,* and *Junyo,* plus the light carrier *Zuiho* - cruised impatiently north of the Solomons waiting for the land battle to begin, the *Enterprise* arrived off Guadalcanal just in the nick of lime. The Big E's battle wounds had been healed by the hard-working Navy Yard repairmen at Pearl Harbor. On her bridge was Rear Admiral Thomas Kinkaid, who became commander of the combined *Hornet-Enterprise* task force. At dawn on October 26, 1942, the two U.S. carriers were prowling off the Santa Cruz Islands southeast of Guadalcanal.

Halsey's orders to Kinkaid, were brief and blunt: "Attack – Repeat —Attack!"

The Battle of the Santa Cruz Islands began with each side sighting the other at almost the same time. Both Kinkaid and Nagumo ordered off heavy air strikes. Kinkaid drew first blood when a pair of his scouting Dauntlesses, after having radioed their sighting, slipped up on the unsuspecting *Zuiho* and dropped two 500-pound bombs on her flight deck. The *Zuiho* had already launched her planes, but no landings could be made on the ruined deck.

The strike force from the *Enterprise* had no luck at all this day, failing to reach the enemy carriers. The pilots from the *Hornet* did better. They tracked down *the Shokaku* and crashed half a dozen bombs into her. With all her planes in the air, Nagumo's flagship was not as vulnerable as the carriers surprised at Midway, and skillful damage control work saved the ship. But the big carrier was out of the war for nine months while she underwent major repairs. The *Junyo* escaped attack, and, as she had done in the Battle of the Coral Sea, the *Zuikaku* found safety under a rain squall.

Meanwhile, Kinkaid's fleet was going through a fiery ordeal. Again as in the Coral Sea action, the U.S. combat air patrol was ineffective, and most of the Vals and Kates got through the fighter screen to attack. Since the *Enterprise* was temporarily hidden by clouds and rain, the first wave concentrated on the *Hornet*.

Over loudspeakers, crewmen in Nagumo's task force heard the leader of the *Shokaku's* dive bombers, Lieutenant Commander Mamoru Seki, radio his pilots: "All planes go in!" Another Val pilot reported later that "Seki's plane seemed to have taken several direct hits soon after he gave the order to attack. . . . I noticed the bomber enter the dive and suddenly begin to roll over on its back. Flame shot out . . . and. still inverted, it continued diving toward the enemy ship."

Commander Seki's Val smashed into the *Hornet's* island, bounced off, and went through the flight deck to the hangar below, where its bombs went off. Four other bombs scored, two ripping deep into the hull before exploding. Two torpedoes hit in the engine rooms, and a second crash-diving bomber rammed into a gun gallery. The carrier drifted to a stop, all power lost, pouring out a huge pillar of smoke.

While the *Hornet* fought for her life, a second wave of Japanese planes discovered the *Enterprise.* The Big E and her escorts put up a tremendous volume of antiaircraft fire that blackened the sky with shellbursts. The battleship *South Dakota* and the new antiaircraft cruiser *San Juan* were especially effective - when the *San Juan* opened up with every gun on board, an American pilot flying overhead thought for a moment the ship had blown up. The defending Wildcats got in their licks too. Fighter pilot Stanley "Swede" Vejtasa, for example, picked off two Vals trying to attack the *Hornet* and later sighted a flight of Kates heading for the *Enterprise.* In a dazzling display of marksmanship, Vejtasa splashed five of the torpedo bombers in a matter of minutes.

Dive bombers twice hit the Big E, starting fires on the hangar deck and damaging the amidships elevator. A near miss close alongside jarred the forward elevator out of line. Captain Osborne Hardison maneuvered the big ship so violently to evade bombs that a Dauntless parked on the flight deck slid off into a gun gallery and another SBD toppled overboard into the sea.

It was not the Vals that gave the crewmen of the Big E their worst moments, however, but rather a well-coordinated attack by Kate torpedo bombers approaching both sides of the carrier at the same time. Those on the starboard (right) side dropped first. Captain Hardison watched the three torpedo tracks for a moment, glanced at the Kates closing in from port, and ordered right full rudder. The drops had been perfect; it was now simply a question of whether the *Enterprise* could turn fast enough.

"Having done all that could be done," reported the ship's historian, "Captain Hardison stood on the port wing of the bridge to witness its success or failure. Admiral Kinkaid came silently to stand beside him." A minute later the bubbling white wakes of the three starboard torpedoes passed down the full length of the ship - ten yards away. The fish dropped by the Kates on the port side missed by a more comfortable thirty yards.

Two more air attacks cost the enemy dozens of planes and caused only slight further damage to the *Enterprise*. By early afternoon, she had her planes as well as those from the *Hornet* aboard, and although badly hurt, was still full of fight. But the Battle of the Santa Cruz Islands was over for the Big E. Admiral Kinkaid ordered her to New Caledonia for repairs.

The *Hornet* made a valiant effort to escape as well. The fires were coming under control, the engineers had somehow restored partial power in the smashed engine rooms, and the heavy cruiser Northampton had the wounded carrier under tow. But Admiral Nagumo's airmen were determined to finish the job they had begun. In mid-afternoon, a Kate from the *Junyo* scored with a torpedo: Later two more bombs hit, and the stricken ship had to be abandoned. Yet, she refused to die. Nine torpedoes and more than 400 shells fired by U.S. destroyers only made the fires burn brighter. Shortly after midnight, Japanese destroyers found the *Hornet* and sent her at last to the bottom.

The Battle of the Santa Cruz Islands was like the Coral Sea fight in a number of ways, including the results. The Japanese squeezed out a narrow edge in the battle itself, but they failed to achieve their overall goals. Once more, as at Midway, Yamamoto saw the major naval victory he dreamed of slip away. On Guadalcanal, the thrust at Henderson Field ended in a bloody repulse. But the Japanese were long on stubbornness. While repair crews at New Caledonia worked desperately on the *Enterprise,* the fight for Guadalcanal grew toward still another climax. The Japanese collected their forces for one last mighty effort to drive the Marines into the sea. From November 12 to November 15, 1942, a series of savage naval actions was fought to decide who would finally control the waters around the island - the side that controlled the sea controlled the supply routes.

The *Enterprise,* scarred but unbowed, steamed into the thick of the fight. She trailed a smear of leaking fuel oil in her wake, and repair crews still welded and hammered as air strikes took off and were recovered. Plane handling was slow because the twisted forward elevator was locked at night deck level; no one dared test it for fear it would jam in the down position and leave the only American carrier in the Pacific helpless.

This November struggle, called the Naval Battle of Guadalcanal, turned the tide at last. American ship losses were heavy, but the Imperial Navy lost two battleships and was driven back. The land battle also went against the Japanese, and a convoy of troopships trying to reach the island with heavy reinforcements was devastated by planes from Henderson Field and the *Enterprise.* The long campaign had cost the Pacific Fleet twenty-four warships, including the carriers *Wasp* and *Hornet,* but no longer was there any doubt about who was going to hold Guadalcanal. In February 1943, the last Japanese troops were withdrawn.

The year just ended had seen the Axis checked everywhere: in North Africa at the Battle of El Alamein, in Russia at the Battle of Stalingrad, in the Pacific at the battles of Midway and Guadalcanal. Since carriers had led the way against the Japanese throughout 1942, the year closed on a particularly fitting note. On December 31, the USS *Essex,* CV-9, was commissioned a warship in the United States Navy.

The *Essex* was the first of a new class of carriers the Navy had ordered even before Pearl Harbor. Close to 900 feet long, the 27,000-ton flattop carried 100 planes, and her defenses included a dozen 5-inchers and nearly 100 rapid-firing lighter guns. In February, 1943, a sister ship joined the fleet, named for the old *Lexington* that had gone down in the Coral Sea. Before the year was out, five more of the big carriers were commissioned: *Intrepid, Bunker Hill,* and three new ships with old names, *Yorktown, Wasp,* and *Hornet.*

These carriers were only a part of the production

miracle achieved by American shipyards. A number of cruisers were hurriedly converted to light carriers during construction, and in 1943, nine of these CVLs were commissioned. In addition to scores of battleships, cruisers, destroyers, submarines, and lesser ships, the shipbuilders produced an astonishing number of small escort carriers (thirty-five of them in 1943 alone). These CVEs were widely used to ferry planes, to patrol against submarines, and to furnish air support for amphibious landings.

The flood of new carriers called for an even greater flood of new planes, and America's aircraft industry met the challenge. The tough, versatile Avenger torpedo bomber began arriving in time to see action in the Guadalcanal campaign, and in mid-1943, a brand-new American carrier fighter plane was introduced into combat.

Even though the gallant Wildcat had dished out a great deal more than it had taken - for every Wildcat lost in combat in 1942, six Japanese planes fell to the F4F's guns - it was clear that a new fighter was needed to match the Zero in flight performance while still surpassing it in firepower and ruggedness. The Grumman F6F Hellcat was the answer. Faster, tougher, more maneuverable, and longer ranged than the Wildcat, the Hellcat was able to beat the agile Zero at its own game. The F6F was designed, tested, and put into production with remarkable speed: The first ones rolled off the assembly lines while the factory was still being built around them.

A second new American fighter, the sleek, gull-winged Vought F4U Corsair, saw action in 1943. Though designed as a carrier fighter, the Corsair went first to Marine land-based squadrons, where it was highly praised for its speed and ruggedness. A new dive bomber, the Curtiss SB2C Helldiver, also went into production during the year. The dependable Dauntless remained in service for some time; however, its fame and reputation was never dimmed by the bigger Helldiver.

All these new ships and new planes did not mean that the Allies had altered their grand strategy, which continued to be centered on Europe. In 1943, the Germans and Italians were thrown out of North Africa; Sicily and Italy were invaded; a build-up continued in England for the invasion of the Continent. What had happened was that America was flexing its mighty industrial muscles and turning out the equipment to fight two wars on opposite sides of the globe at the same time.

There were no carrier-against-carrier battles fought in the Pacific during 1943, primarily because the Imperial Navy was repeatedly caught off balance by American moves; not once did it recover in time to act decisively. As the United States forged new weapons and new strategies, the Japanese slid into defeat and confusion.

With Guadalcanal secured, the next target was Rabaul, the enemy's main base in the Bismarcks. General MacArthur could not advance very far westward on New Guinea with Rabaul and its half-dozen airfields perched menacingly on his right flank. Admiral Halsey's forces began to execute a series of amphibious landings in the Solomons, leapfrogging from island to island toward Rabaul. MacArthur, meanwhile, pushed ahead through New Guinea's sodden jungles and invaded New Britain in the Bismarcks. These two lines of advance formed a giant pincer movement that every day crept closer to the Japanese stronghold.

American carrier forces played no part in the early stages of this approach to Rabaul, but they did benefit indirectly from it. In April 1943, Admiral Yamamoto decided to tour the Solomons to inspect Japanese defenses. As had happened at Midway, Yamamoto was betrayed by leaky security precautions. A broken code revealed his flight schedule to U.S. Intelligence, and long-range Army Lockheed P-38 Lightning fighters ambushed his plane over Bougainville and shot it down in flames. More than any other man, Isoroku Yamamoto was responsible for the excellent training and fighting spirit of the Imperial Navy. He had lost his greatest chance of victory at Midway and had failed to stem the American tide at Guadalcanal, but he fought hard and skillfully, and his death was a severe blow to Japan.

As the U.S. advance continued, hundreds of Japanese carrier planes and pilots were rushed to the defense of Rabaul to operate from its airfields while the carriers returned to Japan to train new air groups. American carrier forces were also regrouping. The crews of the new carriers were vigorously trained by combat veterans, and in September and October 1943, they carried out a series of hit-and-run raids on Japanese island bases. Like the similar raids in early 1942, results were less important than the combat experience gained.

Admiral Nimitz was grooming these fast carrier task forces for a new role. Grand strategy called for not one, but two lines of advance against Japan. Once Rabaul was knocked out, General MacArthur was to continue his push along the northern coast of New Guinea. At the same time, Admiral Nimitz would direct a second offensive straight across the Central Pacific toward Japan. This route was chosen to split and confuse the enemy defenders, to seize bases from which Japan itself could be bombed, and to draw the Imperial Navy into a finish fight.

Most of the islands on Nimitz's target list lay far beyond the range of land-based Allied planes. This new kind of "hit-and-stay offensive," as one historian called it, depended entirely on carrier air power to pound enemy ground defenses, beat down enemy air power, and defend against any attempt by the Imperial Navy to interfere with the landings.

Before the Central Pacific advance got under way, Bill Halsey put in an emergency call for flattops to hit Rabaul, where scouting planes reported a Japanese battle fleet assembling to counterattack the latest American beachhead in the Solomons. On November 5, the carriers responded by sending nearly 100 Avengers, Hellcats, and Dauntlesses swarming over Rabaul, damaging six cruisers and two destroyers and ending any Japanese hopes of an attack on the new Marine beachhead.

Six days later, when the carriers launched a repeat raid on Rabaul, they were heavily counterattacked. The Japanese sent out every plane they could get into the air. "There are millions of 'em!" shouted an American pilot over his radio. "Let's get to work!" Before the attack was over, the fiercely determined fighter pilots, plus the deadly guns of the new CVs *Bunker Hill* and *Essex* and the new CVL Independence, had accounted for some forty Japanese raiders. Eleven U.S. planes were lost.

The flattops then withdrew, leaving Rabaul to land-based planes, and prepared for the first step in the Central Pacific offensive. On November 20, U.S. troops went ashore in the Gilbert Islands. The landings were covered by no less than nineteen aircraft carriers - six fleet types, five CVLs, and eight of the small escort carriers. Japanese air power in the Gilberts and in the Marshalls to the north was savagely battered by Navy planes.

The Gilbert landings were successful, but casualties were high both ashore and at sea. The light carrier *Independence* was badly damaged by a bomber, and the escort carrier *Liscome Bay* was torpedoed by a submarine. The torpedo hit set off stored bombs, and the *Liscome Bay* simply blew apart like a giant firecracker. Flames shot a thousand feet into the air, and pieces of the ship rained down on the decks of a battleship a mile away. The little "jeep" carrier slid under, taking 644 dead with her.

With the initiative firmly in his grip, Admiral Nimitz kept up a relentless pressure. In February 1944, key islands in the Marshalls were taken. Again, carriers shattered the enemy defenses, this time wiping out virtually every Japanese plane based in the large island group.

The Imperial Navy could only look on helplessly from a distance as the Marshalls fell. The bulk of its carrier-plane strength had been chewed up in the Rabaul meat-grinder, while the carriers themselves swung at anchor in home waters waiting for new planes and new air groups. Early in 1944, the Japanese high command withdrew the surviving planes from Rabaul. The battle for the fortress cost the Imperial Navy some 150 carrier planes and about 100 fliers, many of them skilled veterans. Rabaul itself was left to wither, powerless to take any offensive action, its 100,000 troops waiting for an American invasion that never came.

The war news that was once so bright had now turned bitter for the Japanese warlords. The Solomons were lost, and New Guinea was rapidly slipping away under MacArthur's advance. Rabaul's name, as Admiral Halsey remarked, had been changed to Rubble. The Gilberts and the Marshalls were in American hands; the footholds in the Aleutians had been lost. Of the outer defenses of the empire, only Truk in the Carolines remained intact.

Nimitz had plans to change that. In February 1944, he ordered a powerful battle fleet under Vice Admiral Raymond Spruance of Midway fame to go after Truk, a fortress reportedly so strong that it was called the Gibraltar of the Pacific. Spruance's carriers - five CVs and four CVLs - made up Task Force 58, Rear Admiral Marc Mitscher commanding. "They didn't tell us where we were going until we were well on the way," said the leader of the *Essex's* air group. "They announced our destination over the loudspeaker. It was Truk. My first instinct was to jump overboard."

Task force 58 drove in fast on Truk, and on February 17 caught the enemy napping. Admiral Mitscher tried something new, sending his fighters in first to rough up enemy defenses and clear a path for the bombers that followed. The tactic worked perfectly. A total of seventy-two Hellcats howled down out of the dawn sky at Truk's airfields. The Zeros that tried to intercept were shot down, most of them as they struggled for altitude after takeoff. Scores more were wrecked on their fields by strafing Hellcats. When the bombers arrived to complete the job, a squadron commander could not believe his eyes. "I saw only one enemy plane," he said, "and I think he was lost."

That night, the *Enterprise* launched a specially trained Avenger squadron to pay a night visit to Truk. Flying at very low altitude and bombing by radar, the TBFs sent two oil tankers and six merchant ships to the bottom. The next day, the carrier planes mopped up, smashing more ships and destroying harbor installations. Not a single plane rose to intercept. Admiral Spruance completed the humiliation of the Gibraltar of the Pacific by steaming completely around it, his battleships and cruisers sinking several crippled ships that were trying to slip away.

In the summer of 1942, the United States had struggled mightily to collect enough arms and men to launch Operation Watchtower against Guadalcanal. Now, barely eighteen months later, the outer defenses of Japan's Pacific empire had been cracked wide open, and in their devastation of Truk, the fast carrier forces had reached a new peak of skill and power. Little wonder that American carrier-men waited confidently for the supreme test - the day when the Imperial Japanese Navy would come out to fight.

5
TURKEY SHOOT

The aircraft carrier *Taiho* was the pride and joy of the workmen at the Kawasaki Dockyard near Tokyo. Commissioned in March 1944, the 33,000-ton *Taiho* was designed to be the deadliest fighting ship in the Imperial Japanese Navy. Like American Essex-class carriers, she had profited from wartime lessons: a reinforced hull to withstand torpedo damage, very heavy antiaircraft protection, and a flight deck armored with nearly four inches of steel to shrug off bomb hits.

The *Taiho* was also equipped with new planes, as were most of Japan's carriers by 1944. There was a faster, more heavily armed version of the Zero; a new type of torpedo bomber, the Jill, faster and longer ranged than the old Kate; and a dive bomber, called the Judy by the Americans, that was a great improvement over the Val. All in all, the *Taiho* was the equal of the newest American carriers, but she was the only one of her class. In March 1944, the U.S. Pacific Fleet could send into action seven *Essex-class* flattops.

Such odds did not greatly discourage Japan's warlords. Remembering all too well that at Midway the underdog had won, they fell that their re-equipped carrier force, fighting close to home, was ready for one mighty naval battle, a "Japanese Midway," to pull victory out of deepening defeat. This, at any rate, was the hope of Admiral Soemu Toyoda, who became the Imperial Navy's new commander in chief soon after the *Taiho* was commissioned. For the first time since the Guadalcanal campaign, there was the definite prospect of a carrier battle. It remained only for the Americans to make the first move.

The U.S. high command was as eager for a showdown battle as Japan's warlords. One goal of Admiral Nimitz's Central Pacific offensive, in fact, was to lure the Japanese Navy out of hiding. But it took a good deal of effort by Admiral King in Washington before Nimitz's next objective was approved by the war planners. General MacArthur argued that all forces in the Pacific should be thrown into his New Guinea-Philippines line of advance. Admiral King argued that the conquest of the Mariana Islands, some 1,000 miles west of the Marshalls, would yield far greater dividends. Tokyo itself was only 1,500 miles to the north, within range of the new Boeing B-29 Superfortress bombers then rolling off American production lines. B-29s flying from the Marianas, King said, could bring devastation to Japan's home islands far more quickly than anything MacArthur might do in the South Pacific. King won his point, just as he had won his fight to invade Guadalcanal, and in March 1944, orders went out for the capture of the Marianas. The invasion date was set for mid-June.

While the men and equipment needed for an amphibious operation were assembled, Admiral Nimitz exercised his carriers by lending General MacArthur a hand in New Guinea. Fast-moving carrier task forces struck at the Palau and Caroline islands (including a second devastating raid on Truk), destroying hundreds of Japanese planes scheduled for the defense of New Guinea. By June, MacArthur's forces had nearly reached the western tip of New Guinea and would soon be ready for the leap to the Philippines.

In these strikes fighter pilots fresh from training schools learned the vital lessons of combat under the watchful eyes of veterans, and bomber pilots sharpened their aim on Japanese shipping. The airmen learned, too, how much effort the Navy would put into saving their lives.

Ever since the Solomons campaign, the Navy had been perfecting its rescue system. Long-range Catalina flying boats, called "Dumbos" after Walt Disney's flying elephant cartoon character, saved scores of downed airmen. When attacking such distant island targets as Truk, submarines were stationed nearby on "lifeguard duty" to rescue fliers from their life rafts, and seaplanes from the task force's battleships and cruisers patiently searched the area after the raids for the missing. Whenever Dumbo or seaplane crews visited a carrier, they received red-carpet treatment and were fed all the steak and ice cream they could eat.

By June, when the Marianas operation got under way, carrier airmen were sharp and confident, secure in the knowledge that even though they would be a thousand miles from friendly shores, the Navy would spare no effort to rescue them if they were hit. In addition, they had absolute faith in Task Force 58's commander, one of the most popular Americans ever to wear an admiral's stars.

Marc Mitscher had been flying airplanes since 1915, about the time the aircraft carrier was born, and he never strayed far from carriers throughout his long Navy career. In 1928, he made the first takeoff and landing aboard the *Saratoga*. In 1941, he became the old *Hornet's* first captain, commanding her in the Doolittle raid on Japan and at the Battle of

Midway. Mitscher was a small, leathery man who always sat in his "admiral's chair" on the wing of the bridge facing aft so he could watch everything that took place on the flight deck. He looked, said an officer, "like a cherubic hickory nut . . . and spoke so softly that no one ten feet away could hear a word he said." He had a deep affection for those he sent into battle, and he returned with interest the faith his men had in him.

On June 6, 1944 - the same day that Allied forces landed in France to open a new war front against Nazi Germany - the biggest armada so far assembled in the Pacific began moving westward toward the Marianas. Out of its advance base in the Marshalls steamed Mitscher's Task Force 58, with seven fleet carriers and eight CVLs among its 112 ships. The rest of Admiral Raymond Spruance's Fifth Fleet soon followed. All told, the United States was about to hurl 535 ships and 127,000 troops at Japan's inner line of defense.

The enemy's carrier force, now called the First Mobile Fleet, lay at anchor about a thousand miles south of the Marianas. U.S. submarines had torpedoed so many of Japan's tankers that the fleet could no longer count on delivery of enough fuel oil from the Netherlands East Indies if it remained in home waters. Therefore, commander in chief Toyoda ordered his carriers south to a base near the Indies oil supply.

Commander of the First Mobile Fleet was Vice Admiral Jisaburo Ozawa, who had led the conquest of the Indies that he now depended upon for fuel. He had replaced Admiral Nagumo in command of Japan's carrier force after the Battle of the Santa Cruz Islands in 1942. (By coincidence, Nagumo became commander of naval forces in the Marianas. His rickety "fleet" of patrol boats and barges was a sad comedown for the man who had led the attack on Pearl Harbor.) Admiral Ozawa was constantly plagued by U.S. submarines, which picked off several of his destroyers and fleet tankers and made it too dangerous for the carriers to conduct training cruises. This particularly disturbed Ozawa, for few of his pilots had more than six months of flight training, and many of them had a good deal less.

On June 11, Admiral Toyoda received word that the Marianas were being hit hard by U.S. carrier planes, and he issued orders for a major counterattack on the Pacific Fleet. On June 13, Ozawa's First Mobile Fleet put out to sea, heading northward. The admiral passed on to every ship in the force a message from the commander in chief: "The fate of the Empire rests on this one battle. Every man is expected to do his utmost." The same message was delivered before the Battle of Tsushima in 1905, when the Imperial Navy had utterly destroyed a larger Russian fleet.

Part of Toyoda's plan immediately went off

the rails when Admiral Mitscher caught the Marianas' defenders napping. Toyoda's scheme called for land-based air power on the three main islands - Saipan, Guam, and Tinian - to knock out a third of the U.S. carriers; instead, it was Mitscher's fighters and bombers that delivered the knockout. They also worked over the Volcano Islands to the north, where air reinforcements were stationed. When the Marines fought their way ashore on Saipan on June 15, Japanese air power in the Marianas was crippled.

By this time, Mitscher knew that the Imperial Navy was coming out to do battle, for shadowing submarines had reported the speed, course, and size of Ozawa's force. The last of these reports, on June 17, placed the enemy fleet in the Philippine Sea a few hundred miles west of the Marianas; then the subs lost contact. Mitscher proposed to Admiral Spruance that Task Force 58 set out at full speed after the Japanese.

Spruance, however, had a number of problems to consider. For one thing, Ozawa's fleet was not definitely located. For another, Task Force 58's first responsibility was to protect the Marine beachhead on Saipan and the vulnerable transports and cargo ships supplying it. In every carrier battle fought so far, the Japanese had attempted such tricky tactics as bait ships or flanking movements. Spruance had to guard against an "end run" by part of the Japanese fleet that could pounce on the landing forces like wolves on sheep if Task Force 58 was lured off to the west. In the early morning hours of June 19, he reluctantly ordered Mitscher to stand by the beachhead until the enemy was definitely located.

This was exactly what Admiral Ozawa had been counting on. His battle plan was both simple and shrewd. Japanese carrier planes, lacking armor and self-sealing gas tanks, were lighter and therefore longer ranged than American types. On June 19, Ozawa intended to lie just out of reach of American planes and launch a maximum air strike at Mitscher's carriers. Using the Guam airfields to rearm and refuel his planes, he would hit the U.S. fleet coming and going. By bringing Task Force 58 under fire from two directions, and by staying out of range of a counterattack, the Japanese admiral hoped to cut American strength down to size.

Ozawa needed every advantage he could get, for he was badly outnumbered. In addition to his flagship *Taiho*, he had four other fleet carriers - *Hiyo, Junyo,* and the veterans *Shokaku* and *Zuikaku* - and four light carriers to pit against Mitscher's fifteen flattops. Japanese air strength totaled 430 fighters, dive bombers, and torpedo planes. Aboard the American carriers were 891 planes, including 475 Hellcat fighters.

Sunrise on June 19 found Task Force 58 cruising

impatiently west of the Marianas. The weather was warm and pleasant, the sky bright, with visibility unlimited, A dawn patrol of Avengers ranged off to the west looking for the elusive enemy. Hellcats from the CVL *Belleau Wood* checked Guam, found its airfield buzzing with activity, and opened the day's fighting. Other F6Fs joined the fray over Guam, and before long they had accounted for thirty-five Japanese planes.

American search planes found nothing, but the Japanese dawn patrol made several sightings of Mitscher's task force. At 8:30 a.m., Ozawa ordered off his planes. At a few minutes after nine, as his flagship *Taiho* was launching the last of her bombers, lookouts sighted two torpedo wakes. Warrant Officer Sakio Komatsu had just taken off when he saw them too. With no hesitation, he dove his plane into the sea, blowing up one torpedo and himself with it. But the second fish bored straight on toward the *Taiho* as Ozawa watched helplessly. It hit near the forward gasoline tanks; the *Taiho* lurched sharply and then raced on smoothly at twenty-six knots. The workmen at the Kawasaki Dockyard had done their job well.

The torpedoes were from the American submarine *Albacore.* Her captain, Commander James Blanchard, had sighted the juicy target through his periscope, but then the automatic computer by which he aimed his torpedoes broke down. Blanchard fired six fish anyway, aiming by eye. He heard one hit as he crash-dived to avoid enemy destroyers. Sadly he reported only "probable damage."

At ten o'clock, radar screens in the American fleet filled with unidentified blips, range 150 miles. On board his flagship *Lexington*, Admiral Mitscher himself picked up a microphone and called the Hellcats back from Guam with the old circus cry "Hey, Rube!" that meant trouble was brewing. The carriers turned into the wind and launched wave after wave of fighters. The dive bombers and torpedo planes were sent aloft with orders to stay clear of the fight.

The leading element of Ozawa's striking force was made up almost entirely of Zeros, sixty-one of them. He apparently hoped they would keep the American interceptors occupied while the second wave, mostly bombers, slipped through to attack the U.S. ships. (Here again was that favorite Japanese trick, the bait force.) Hellcats from the *Essex* were the first to spot the enemy planes.

Air combat was so fast that a fighter pilot had to make decisions in split seconds and needed to do a variety of things at once: maneuver his plane with control stick, rudder pedals, and throttle; check his instruments for telltale danger signs such as rising engine temperature or dropping oil pressure; peer into his gunsight when he maneuvered into firing position; and most important, constantly search the sky in every direction. There was an old saying among fighter pilots that "you never see the plane that shoots you down."

As far as a fighter pilot was concerned, ideal attack position was directly behind the enemy plane. This gave him a "no-deflection" shot: Since both planes were going in the same direction, he simply aimed straight at the enemy and fired. A "full-deflection" shot, on the other hand, was needed when attacking from the side, at right angles to the opponent: The pilot had to "lead" the other plane just the right amount so that it flew into the path of his bullets. His gun sight helped him to figure out this problem, but any pilot who scored on a full-deflection shot was usually a crack marksman.

All of this, of course, could only be learned by training and practice. The U.S. Navy took about two years to train a pilot, and at the beginning of the war, Japanese carrier airmen were equally well trained. But the Imperial Navy was slow to expand its training program, and after the heavy losses at Midway, Guadalcanal, and Rabaul, it never caught up. Nor had the Zero's designers been able to catch up. The new model, particularly with a green pilot at the controls, was simply no match for the Hellcat. These facts were apparent as Ozawa's strike force tangled with Mitscher's interceptors.

The leader of the *Essex's* Fighting 15, Lieutenant Commander C. W. Brewer, roared down on the Japanese flight leader's Zero and blew it to pieces with a short burst that hit its gas tank. Brewer quickly sent two more fighters into the sea and then found himself in a twisting, turning dogfight with a skillful enemy pilot. He kept his F6F glued to the Zero's tail through a spectacular series of violent maneuvers, firing short bursts that knocked pieces off the Japanese fighter. Finally, his bullets touched off its vulnerable gas tank, and the Zero fell into a tight, flaming spin.

By this time, scores of Hellcats from other carriers had joined the battle. "The air was so clear that you could see planes tangling in the sky," said a *Lexington* officer. "Then a flamer would go down. We would hope it was a Jap, and from the radio chatter we could hear from the pilots, it seemed that the Japs were getting the worst end of it." More than half the raiders were shot down long before they reached the carriers. The only damage to the fleet was a single bomb hit on the battleship *South Dakota*, killing twenty-seven men. One Hellcat was lost.

After a brief pause in the fighting, radar picked up a second and much bigger raid coming in. This was Ozawa's Sunday punch - 109 fighters and bombers from *Taiho, Shokaku,* and *Zuikaku,* his biggest carriers. Instead of finding their path cleared by the first wave of fighters, the enemy airmen saw only blue Hellcats everywhere they looked.

Lieutenant Alex Vraciu had "scrambled" with the rest of the *Lexington's* pilots early in the fight, but his engine acted up and would not develop full power. The fighter director radioed him to circle over the fleet until new targets were sighted. Vraciu had once been a wingman of the famous Edward "Butch" O'Hare, the Navy's first carrier hero. O'Hare had taught Vraciu a great deal about combat flying, and when he was shot down and killed during the Gilbert Islands campaign, Vraciu swore to avenge his death. He had made a good start - twelve kills up to June 19 - but the balky engine left him gloomy over his chances in this action.

Finally, the fighter director gave him a bearing on a new Japanese formation. Soon he sighted at least fifty planes far below, the red disks on their wings standing out vividly. Vraciu joined a swarm of other Hellcats heading full tilt for the enemy.

Vraciu came out of his dive to pour bullets into a dive bomber, blowing it up. "Scratch one Judy!" he shouted into his microphone. He then lined up behind a three-plane formation of Judys and knocked them down one after another like tenpins. "After we had been on them a few minutes they began to separate like a bunch of disorderly cattle," Vraciu reported later. "Every time one of the Japs would try to lead a string of others out of formation the Hellcat pilots turned into 'cowboys' and herded them back into the group. . . ." He caught up to another three-plane element just as it reached its diving point over the American fleet. His machine guns chewed apart the first of the Judys and set off the bomb of the second one, which disappeared in a brilliant yellow flash. A battleship's antiaircraft guns got the third dive bomber.

It was the custom for a carrier pilot to signal the number of his victories as he taxied up the deck after landing. With a huge grin on his face, Vraciu held up six fingers for the men on the *Lexington's* bridge to see. When he climbed out of his cockpit, he found Admiral Mitscher himself waiting to shake his hand.

Only about twenty planes out of Ozawa's Sunday punch evaded American fighters and antiaircraft fire to go after Task Force 58. Bombs narrowly missed the carriers *Wasp* and *Bunker Hill*, a torpedo exploded harmlessly in the *Enterprise's* wake, and a burning Jill torpedo plane crashed into the hull of the battleship *Indiana*. The impact did not even dent the *Indiana's* 18 eighteen-inch thick belt of armor. These trifling results cost Admiral Ozawa over ninety planes.

By now noon had passed, and Ozawa was growing worried. Radio reports from his strike pilots were few and garbled; "the silence was mystifying and disturbing," wrote a Japanese historian. At 12:20, the admiral was shocked to see three tall fountains of water, blackened by oil and debris, erupt alongside the fleet carrier *Shokaku.* The carrier slewed to a stop, listing and on fire, the victim of torpedoes fired by the U.S. submarine *Cavalla.*

As the *Shokaku* burned, the battle over Task Force 58 blazed up again. A third wave of Japanese planes, mostly Zeros, had finally sighted its quarry after wandering around lost for over an hour. They were driven off by the ever-alert Hellcats before they could make any attacks. A fourth wave had even less luck, most of the eighty-two planes completely missing the American force and heading for Guam.

For the Japanese, this day of disaster now reached a climax. The *Shokaku*'s damage-control parties seemed to have her fires under control, but at 3:00 p.m., the submariners in the *Cavalla,* sweating out depth-charge attacks far below, had the satisfaction of hearing "four terrific explosions from the direction of the carrier. . . . Their rumblings continued for many seconds." The *Shokaku*'s bomb and torpedo magazines had exploded. The big carrier broke up quickly and went to the bottom of the Philippine Sea.

Not long afterward, a damage-control officer aboard the *Taiho* decided to get rid of the annoying fumes from a tank of aviation gasoline damaged by the *Albacore*'s single torpedo hit six hours before. He turned on the ship's ventilating system full blast to blow away the fumes. The result, however, was just the opposite of what the young officer had intended. Deadly gasoline fumes spread into every compartment of the big carrier, and a spark, probably from a generator motor, set them off.

"Suddenly a terrible explosion burst the flight deck into the shape of a mountain top," reported a Japanese sailor. Not only did the blast turn the armored deck into scrap metal, but it also blew gaping holes in the hull and killed every man in the engine rooms. In minutes, the *Taiho* was aflame from stem to stern. A lifeboat took Admiral Ozawa to a waiting destroyer. Two hours later, the mighty *Taiho*, whose planes had fought only one battle and that a losing one - rolled over and sank with 1,650 of her crew.

Although the day's action is officially known as a part of the Battle of the Philippine Sea, a *Lexington* fighter pilot gave it a more descriptive name. To him it had been as rewarding - and nearly as safe - as a turkey shoot back home, and so the great air battle of June 19, 1944, came to be known as the Marianas Turkey Shoot.

By whatever name, the battle wrecked the Imperial Navy's carefully hoarded carrier air power. At dawn on June 19, Admiral Ozawa could count 430 combat planes aboard his nine carriers. At dawn on June 20, he had only 100 planes and seven carriers left. American losses for the day, both combat and accidental, totaled twenty-nine planes. No more one-sided air battle was fought in the entire course of World War II.

At the time, however, the American carrier-men were not in a very good humor over the whole affair. They had shot down a great many Japanese planes, and the submarine *Cavalla* had reported sinking a big carrier (the *Taiho's* loss was not yet known), but Task Force 58 planes had not attacked a single Japanese ship. What was worse, they had failed even to sight the First Mobile Fleet. Throughout the day and night of June 19, a "Japanese wind" blew from east to west, forcing Mitscher to head away from the enemy every time he launched or recovered planes. Evening found him farther from his quarry than he had been at dawn.

For his part, Admiral Ozawa was not entirely discouraged. His battle plan had certainly worked well enough, for no enemy plane had yet "snooped" his fleet. His pilots brought back excited reports of seeing as many as four American carriers sinking. He had no idea of his air losses, thinking most of the missing planes were safe on Guam. He planned to recover them from the island and resume the battle.

On the afternoon of June 20, the situation changed radically for both sides. Ozawa picked the *Zuikaku* as his new flagship and boarded her. There he learned the terrible truth - Guam had not a single one of his planes in flying condition. Then, shortly before 4:00 p.m., Ozawa's last bit of luck deserted him. The First Mobile Fleet was located by an American search plane.

The sighting was radioed back to Task Force 58, and Admiral Mitscher and his staff gathered around the chart table in the *Lexington*'s flag plot. Commander Gus Widhelm, the air operations officer, whistled in dismay when the Japanese position was marked on the map. "Well, can we make it?" Mitscher asked him. "We can make it, but it's going to be tight," Widhelm answered after a pause. "Launch 'em!" Mitscher ordered.

Although he knew he had no real choice, this was an extremely hard decision for Mitscher to make. His opponent was some 300 miles away, at the very limit of the combat range of American planes. There would be little or no "safety margin" of gasoline for full-power combat maneuvering over the enemy fleet. Also, a strike force launched so late in the day would have to be recovered after dark; few of the pilots were trained in night landings, and all of them would be exhausted after the long flight. This knowledge was a heavy burden for a man who felt about his airmen as a father feels about his sons.

In their ready rooms, the fliers gasped at the briefing instructions. They located the enemy position almost in the margin of the navigation chartboards they carried, and there was little of the usual joking and horseplay as they filed out to man their planes. In the remarkably short time of ten minutes, Task Force 58 launched 216 Hellcats, Dauntlesses, Avengers, and Helldivers. Mitscher then set a high-speed course toward the enemy to shorten the distance his men would have to fly on their return.

Shortly after 6:30, the Japanese carriers were sighted, framed against a spectacular sunset. Zeros rose to intercept, and a *Bunker Hill* airman saw antiaircraft shells burst in an array of colors - "blue, yellow, lavender, pink, red, white, and black. Some bursts threw out sparkling incendiary particles; some dropped phosphorous-appearing streamers." Ozawa may have been short of planes, but he had plenty of antiaircraft ammunition. So rapid were the gun flashes that the ships looked as if they were on fire.

The *Enterprise* and the *Lexington* were the only Task Force 58 carriers whose Dauntlesses had not yet been replaced by Helldivers; ironically, the reliable old SBDs gave a better account of themselves than the new dive bombers. Dauntless pilots from the Big E scored several hits on the light carrier *Ryuho* and were particularly pleased to put bombs into their old opponent, the *Zuikaku*. After *Yorktown* and *Hornet* Avengers added several hits, severe fires broke out on the hangar deck. But the *Zuikaku* had led a charmed life in the Pacific battles, and she still had some luck left. Although the abandon ship order was given at one point during the fight to save her, the crew put on a superhuman effort and brought the fires under control.

The Avengers also did well. One TBF pilot, carrying bombs instead of a torpedo, tore up the whole after section of a light carrier's flight deck. Another TBF, flown by Lieutenant George Brown of the *Belleau Wood,* was hit during a torpedo run at the fleet carrier *Hiyo.* The Avenger caught fire, and the radioman and the gunner had to bail out, but Brown was wounded and stayed with the plane; luckily the fire burned itself out. Brown released his torpedo and then Hew close alongside the carrier to draw the fire of her gunners. While they blazed away at him, two more Avengers slipped in almost unnoticed to drop their deadly fish. Two of the three torpedoes hit. Later, one of his squadron mates caught up with Brown flying slowly away from the battle. He could see him slumped in his cockpit, his shirt covered with blood. Then Brown's TBF flew into a cloud and was never seen again.

The outnumbered Zeros fought skillfully, and it was obvious that only the best of the Japanese pilots had escaped the Turkey Shoot of the previous day. "Looking back," said an *Enterprise* pilot, "the sky was a mass of bursting shells, flaming planes, and the Hellcats and Zeros still fighting it out above." Twenty of the American attackers were shot down, but Admiral Ozawa's losses were sixty-five. His toll for the two-day battle had now reached the staggering figure of 395 carrier planes.

In the gathering twilight, the torpedoed *Hiyo* blazed fiercely. Several downed American fliers, including Lieutenant Brown's two crewmen, witnessed her death agonies from their rubber rafts. The flight deck burned completely away, and a drumfire of explosions rocked the ship. Soon, the watchers saw the great propellers heave out of the water as she settled rapidly by the bow; then the glowing hulk went under with a great hissing sound. The Battle of the Philippine Sea had claimed a third Japanese aircraft carrier.

For the American raiders, the worst of their ordeal still lay before them. The hard fight over the enemy fleet had used up a great deal of gasoline, and most gauges registered less than half full as the planes turned eastward toward Task Force 58. Gunners closed their canopies to cut down wind resistance, and pilots slowed down their engine as much as they dared to save gas.

Before long, planes began to drop out of formation, the pilots electing to ditch in the ocean while they still had gas left for a controlled, powered landing. A group of five Helldiver pilots took a vote by radio and decided to ditch together, and a few minutes later, other crews saw splashes far below, dim in the growing darkness, as the planes went in. Most fliers, however, decided to use their last gallons of fuel to get as close to home as possible. About seventy-five miles from the task force, they began picking up the "homing signal" over their radios. By this time, it was pitch black, and the signal was insurance that at least they would not fly off in the wrong direction entirely. If they had to ditch now, their chances of being sighted by search planes the next day would be fairly good.

At about 8:30 p.m., the men in Task Force 58 began to hear planes circling overhead. Over the loudspeakers came the anxious voices of pilots: "Hello, any station! Any station! Where am I, please? Can somebody tell me where I am?" As it always did at night, the fleet was blacked out and maintaining radio silence to avoid giving away its position to prowling Japanese planes and submarines. Only five nights before, despite these precautions, the flagship *Lexington* had narrowly avoided four torpedoes dropped by raiders from the Marianas. And during the strike at Truk in February, the fleet carrier *Intrepid* had been heavily damaged by a Japanese torpedo bomber in a nighttime assault.

Marc Mitscher prowled restlessly between the bridge and flag plot, looking up at the sky, hearing the engines overhead, listening to his pilots. Finally, he sat down in flag plot, lit a cigarette, and smoked in silence for several minutes. Then he looked at his chief of staff and said quietly, "Turn on the lights."

"We heard a commotion topside," reported a *Lexington* officer. "We piled up to the deck - and the lights were on. Not the dim lights that reveal the paddles of the man signaling the pilots in, but the floodlights. Not only running lights, but searchlights hitting the sky. Men were dancing around and hugging each other like crazy [and] the ships were even sending up starshells."

Mitscher radioed his pilots to land on any carrier they could find. When the lights came on, the fliers immediately headed for the largest carriers, figuring that they stood a better chance of landing safely on a big flight deck than on the smaller decks of the light carriers. The result was a nightmare for the landing officers on the fleet carriers. They found two, three, even half a dozen planes roaring down on them at once, jockeying for position, desperately trying to get aboard before their tanks ran dry. Five times the *Lexington's* signalman John Shuff had to dive into his safety net to avoid low-flying planes that only took his wave-offs at the last possible moment.

Crash landings were frequent, and when one of these accidents left a carrier's deck "fouled," the lights were turned off until the wreckage was cleared away. Pilots then "shopped around" the fleet for a clear flight deck or ditched as close to a ship as possible when their fuel ran out. The

Enterprise landed fighters and bombers for half an hour before one of her own planes finally came aboard. A few minutes later, a Hellcat landed, and its tail hook caught the fifth arrester wire, well forward. A Dauntless was right on the fighter's tail, and before the signal officer could give the SBD a wave-off, it too landed. Its tail hook caught the second wire. The Big E had landed two planes at almost the same instant without either one being so much as scratched.

The flagship *Lexington* was not so lucky. A Helldiver had just landed, and deck crewmen were folding its wings as it taxied into a parking spot forward when a second Helldiver came in much too fast and ignored landing-officer Shuff's frantic wave-off. It missed the arrester gear completely and slashed into the Helldiver being parked, killing its rear gunner instantly, crushing a deckman, and injuring six men. Three other parked planes were demolished in the crash. After the casualties were removed, a crane tugged apart the twisted wreckage and dropped it over the side. In ten minutes, the *Lexington*'s lights were on, and she was recovering planes.

The pilot of the second Helldiver was helped into one of the ready rooms. His plane had been badly damaged, and he had been wounded in the attack; now he was nearly hysterical with grief. At a doctor's gentle urging, he told what had happened. "I found this carrier, but the landing circle was jammed," he explained. "I didn't have but a handful of gas left and no lights. I couldn't have made it around again. I knew I couldn't. I pushed my way into the circle. I saw the wave-off, but I couldn't make myself take it, I just couldn't . . . I wish to God I had, now. I'd give anything . . . Those men I killed . . ."

Lieutenant Cook Cleland was twice waved off trying to land on the light carrier Princeton, four times waved off big carriers, and very nearly landed on top of a destroyer whose lights looked like a carrier's. He finally touched down on the *Enterprise*, and as a deckman motioned him forward to park, his engine died, out of gas. Cleland's Dauntless had huge holes in one wing, another in the fuselage, and the tail was riddled. The deck captain wanted to push it over the side, but Cleland had literally made it back on a wing and a prayer, and he threatened to shoot the first man who laid a hand on his beloved SBD, It stayed aboard.

The wild evening reached a climax when the light carrier *San Jacinto* insisted there was a Japanese Jill torpedo bomber trying to come aboard. Three times the Jill appeared out of the darkness, each time obediently obeying the wave-off of the flabbergasted signal officer. The Jill was then reported to have tried both the *Bunker Hill* and the *Enterprise,* with the same result, before disappearing. The story had many doubters, and there was no way to prove its truth, but the men of the *San Jacinto* could never be convinced that they had just been seeing things.

During the two hours that Admiral Mitscher kept Task Force 58 lit up like Times Square on New Year's Eve, well over half the planes of the strike force landed safely. Eighty either ditched or were wrecked in landing accidents. The sea around the ships was dotted with life rafts, their flashing lights looking like fireflies on a summer night. Destroyers darted about, sweeping the surface with searchlights and rescuing airmen by the dozens. The next day search planes and ships scoured the whole area. Float planes from the battleships and cruisers even picked up the men who had bailed out or ditched during the attack on the Japanese fleet, which had long since fled to safety.

Thanks to these prompt rescue efforts - and Mitscher's decision to turn on the lights - all but forty-nine of the 209 airmen downed in combat or ditched near the task force were saved. On this happy note, the Battle of the Philippine Sea, the greatest carrier clash of the war, became part of history.

6
DEATH OF A NAVY

Stephen W. Sears

When Admiral Jisaburo Ozawa ordered his battered First Mobile Fleet to make best speed westward on the night of June 20, 1944, he was doing more than just admitting the failure of the Imperial Navy's counterattack. His defeat in the Battle of the Philippine Sea gave the United States control of the sea around and the air above the Marianas. It cost over 5,600 American lives to conquer the islands, but with the defenders cut off from reinforcement, the outcome was never in doubt. On November 24, the first B-29 Superfortresses roared down Tinian's runway and headed north to bomb Japan.

The loss of the Marianas, combined with the slaughter of the Imperial Navy's carrier air power, was a staggering blow to Japan. General Tojo was forced to resign as head of the government, and Emperor Hirohito urged his officials to find a way to end the fighting. But the Japanese military leaders could not bear the humiliating "loss of face" of coming to terms with an enemy. Nothing was done to seek peace. As far as the United States knew, Japan intended to fight on to the bitter, bloody end.

With the situation in the Marianas under control, the problem for America's war planners during the summer of 1944 was where to go next. MacArthur, of course, pressed for the liberation of the Philippines. Others wanted to take the big island of Formosa, off China, or seize a beachhead on the Chinese coast, or even invade Japan itself. It was finally decided that Mindanao, the southernmost island of the Philippines, would be invaded in mid-November.

While grand strategy was being debated, Bill Halsey took his turn as commander of the Pacific Fleet's main fighting force. Halsey and Spruance were to trade off - while one fought, the other would make plans and supervise training for the next operation. "The team remains about the same, but the drivers change," said Admiral Nimitz. Under Spruance, the team was called the Fifth Fleet, spearheaded by the carriers of Task Force 58; under Halsey it became the Third Fleet and Task Force 38. Marc Mitscher remained in command of the carriers.

Halsey immediately sent Task Force 38 fliers roaming over the Philippines to beat down Japanese air power. Much to his surprise, there was almost no resistance. Halsey was a stand-up, slug-it-out fighter, and he could see no sense to a slow, cautious climb "up the ladder" in the Philippines if the enemy might be faltering.

He urged that all planned operations be canceled; he proposed instead that Leyte, an island in the very heart of the Philippines, be invaded on October 20, just five weeks away.

A major speed-up in the Pacific timetable was quickly approved along the lines suggested by Halsey. The conquest of two advance bases, Morotai and the Palau Islands, went ahead as scheduled, but everything else was directed toward the invasion of Leyte. Seizing Leyte would give the United States air bases from which to smother the rest of the Philippines; U.S. planes could also range far out over the South China Sea, through which Japan's oil tankers and merchantmen passed on their voyages between the home islands and the conquered lands of the Netherlands East Indies and Southeast Asia. In short, Americans on Leyte would menace Japan's lifeline to its southern empire just as two years before, Japanese on Guadalcanal had threatened America's lifeline to the South Pacific.

To "run interference" for the Leyte invasion, Mitscher's Task Force 38 was divided into four task groups. Task Group 1 was under Vice Admiral John McCain, a long-time Navy flier in his first carrier command. Rear Admiral Gerald Bogan, who was in charge of an escort carrier group in the Marianas operation, had TG-2. Rear Admiral Frederick Sherman, carrier veteran and captain of the old *Lexington* when she went down in the Battle of the Coral Sea, had TG-3. TG-4 was Rear Admiral Ralph Davison's; like Bogan, he was a former escort carrier group commander. Each task group was built around two fleet carriers and two light carriers.

Early in October, 1944, Task Force 38 steamed out of its new advanced base at Ulithi in the Carolines to nip off Japanese air and naval reinforcements for the Philippines. Mitscher's planes hit the Ryukyu Islands, only 350 miles south of Japan, then pounded airfields in the Philippines and on Formosa, and finally raided the Philippines again. The results were spectacular, with over 600 Japanese planes destroyed in the Formosa battle alone.

On October 20, 1944, General MacArthur's troops poured ashore on Leyte. For Douglas MacArthur this was the proudest day of a proud military career. In March 1942, he had been ordered out of the Philippines by President Roosevelt, leaving behind on Bataan his doomed army of Americans and Filipinos. Then he had vowed, "I shall return"; now, a little more than two and a half years later, he strode ashore on Leyte, his pledge redeemed. "Rally to me," he told the Filipinos. "Let the indomitable spirit of Bataan and Corregidor lead on."

MacArthur was backed by a massive array of air power and gun power supplied by the U.S. Navy. In Leyte Gulf, off the beachhead, was the Seventh Fleet - landing and supply vessels, covered by a force of old battleships and small escort carriers - under Vice Admiral Thomas Kinkaid, who had commanded the *Enterprise-Hornet* force in the Battle of the Santa Cruz Islands back in 1942. In the Philippine Sea to the east was Halsey's Third Fleet, pared down now to little more than Task Force 38 in order to loan the Seventh Fleet additional fire power for the beachhead. Mitscher had three carrier task groups (McCain's TG-1 was on its way to Ulithi to replenish supplies) to keep down Japanese air power in the Philippines and guard against any counterstroke by the Imperial Navy.

This new American offensive once again caught the Imperial Navy off balance. Admiral Ozawa's carrier force was in the Inland Sea of Japan, where desperate efforts were being made to obtain new planes and train new airmen. Ozawa had hoped the Americans would not strike before November, when he might have enough carrier planes and pilots to meet them. But he was not given the time;

in addition, many of the airmen he had collected were ordered to Formosa to meet Task Force 38's pre-Leyte strikes. Most of these half-trained fliers were lost.

Admiral Soemu Toyoda, commander in chief of the Imperial Navy, had stationed a large part of his fleet at Singapore, in Southeast Asia, to be near oil supplies. Toyoda knew well enough that if the Philippines were lost, his supply lines would be cut; little or no fuel oil could reach the carriers in home waters, nor could ammunition and other supplies reach the ships at Singapore. Toyoda had no choice: His fleet must fight now, or it could never fight again.

Admiral Toyoda had in mind a huge pincers movement to crush MacArthur's naval support in Leyte Gulf, leaving the general and his men stranded in the beachhead. The complex plan required three fleets. The Southern Force, composed of two battleships and something over a dozen cruisers and destroyers, was drawn from both Japan and Singapore. The Center Force, sailing from Singapore, included five battleships and ten heavy cruisers, plus assorted light cruisers and destroyers. From Japan came the Northern Force, made up of four carriers and two battleships, plus escorts.

The Southern Force was to slip up on Leyte Gulf from the south through Surigao Strait. The Center

Force under Vice Admiral Takeo Kurita was to pass through San Bernardino Strait north of Leyte and curl around to form the second prong of the pincers. The most powerful of the three fleets, it included the super-battleships *Musashi* and *Yamato*, 68,000-ton monsters that each mounted nine 18.1-inch guns (the largest U.S. battleships were of the 45,000-ton *Iowa* class, with 16-inch guns). Their huge naval rifles fired a 3,200-pound shell, and each of their gun turrets weighed as much as a big destroyer.

In contrast to Kurita's powerful Center Force, the Northern Force was a "paper tiger." Ozawa scraped together woefully understrength air groups to man four carriers: the veteran *Zuikaku* and the CVLs *Chiyoda*, *Zuiho*, and *Chitose*. His two old battleships had short flight decks in place of their after gun turrets, but there were no planes or pilots for them. Admiral Ozawa, a tough, proud sailor, had the distasteful job of being bait for a trap. He was to lure Halsey's Third Fleet away from Leyte Gulf so that the Center and Southern forces could attack the beachhead without interference. Ozawa sortied from Japan expecting to sacrifice all his ships.

By the time General MacArthur had gone ashore on Leyte, all the various Japanese forces were on the move. In the early hours of October 23, the U.S. submarines *Darter* and *Dace*, patrolling west of the Philippines, picked up a large formation of heavy ships on their radars. They tracked the force, radioed their sighting to Halsey and Kinkaid, and then struck at dawn, sending two of the Center Force's heavy cruisers to the bottom and crippling a third. The next day both the Center and Southern forces were sighted by U.S. planes, and the Battle of Leyte Gulf was on.

Within the next forty-eight hours, the greatest naval battle in history was fought. It involved four separate actions and nearly every class of warship imaginable, from submarines and plywood motor-torpedo boats to great aircraft carriers and battleships. There were air strikes and torpedo assaults, daytime and nighttime clashes, big-gun duels and suicide attacks. And enough controversy was generated to keep armchair strategists arguing to this day.

As soon as the approaching Japanese forces were located, Halsey ordered the Task Force 38 carriers to launch air strikes. Before Admiral Sherman's Task Group 3 could send off its planes, however, it was attacked by a swarm of Japanese bombers and fighters from the Philippines. Sherman's combat air patrol began intercepting the attackers long before they reached their targets. Commander David McCampbell, leader of the *Essex* air group, and his wingman, Lieutenant Roy Rushing, spotted some three dozen Japanese fighters thirty miles from

TG-3 and unhesitatingly attacked. McCampbell had splashed two Zeros and Rushing one when the rest formed a tight defensive circle. The two Hellcat pilots climbed above the circling planes "to light a cigarette and await further developments." Finally, the Zeros, low on fuel, gave up their circle and headed back to the Philippines. McCampbell and Rushing pounced on them.

"It was simply a question of watching for an opening," McCampbell said. Time after time he and his wingman dived on the enemy formation. The Japanese pilots made only weak efforts to evade them, and McCampbell finally had to make pencil marks on his instrument panel to keep track of his score. After shooting down six, Lieutenant Rushing ran out of ammunition. The more experienced McCampbell, who had fought on the old *Wasp* in 1942 and had piled up seven victories in the Battle of the Philippine Sea, fired sparingly. Before his guns went silent, he knocked down nine Zeros and damaged two others.

Other sharpshooting Hellcat pilots of the TG-3 combat air patrol shot down or turned back all the rest of the Japanese planes but one. A Judy dive bomber swooped out of a cloud and put a 550-pound bomb through the flight deck of the light carrier *Princeton*. The explosion started gasoline fires in several Avengers on the hangar deck, and then the torpedoes in the TBFs went off.

With a rending crash, both elevators were blown out of the flight deck. Fire spread quickly.

For six hours, the men of the *Princeton* fought for her life. But in mid-afternoon, with the light cruiser *Birmingham* alongside to help in the fire-fighting, flames licked into the torpedo magazine. Most of the carrier's stern was blown off, and the *Birmingham* was riddled with lethal fragments that killed 241 men and injured another 418. The *Princeton* was now beyond saving and had to be sunk.

Admiral Sherman had finally managed to launch his air strike, but in the meantime, bombers from the task groups under Admirals Bogan and Davison were pounding the Japanese Center Force in the Sibuyan Sea in the central Philippines. With most of the Japanese land-based planes out after Sherman's carriers, Admiral Kurita had almost no air cover. His ships put up a heavy barrage of antiaircraft fire, the battleships and cruisers even firing main batteries at their aerial tormentors. Nearly all of Kurita's ships were attacked, but the favorite target was the *Musashi*. The huge battleship was hit repeatedly, until Hell-divers had scored with seventeen bombs and Avengers with nineteen torpedoes. The *Musashi* reeled under the blows, settling deep in the water and listing sharply; that evening she rolled over and sank.

Reports reaching Admiral Halsey on the Battle of

the Sibuyan Sea were enthusiastic. The airmen had seen one bomb and torpedo after another strike home. Ships were afire and steaming in aimless circles. Before darkness hid it, the Center Force was seen to reassemble, turn away from San Bernardino Strait, and head back the way it had come.

Admiral Halsey had a second interesting piece of news to ponder. Shortly before 5:00 p.m., *Lexington* search planes sighted enemy carriers well to the north. This was Admiral Ozawa's bait force, and for a time, the admiral was worried that no one would find him to take the bait. He had his ships make heavy smoke and break radio silence in an effort to give himself away: The American scout planes were a welcome sight.

Bill Halsey had to make a fast decision. Four Japanese carriers were located, and from all the information available to him, they now seemed to be the most dangerous threat to the Leyte beachhead. The Center Force had been heavily attacked and appeared to be retreating. The Southern Force, tracked and counted, looked as if it could be easily handled by the battleships of Kinkaid's Seventh Fleet in Leyte Gulf. So, at 8:00 p.m. on October 24, Halsey set out after Ozawa with all his ships except McCain's Task Group I, still returning from its interrupted trip to Ulithi. He radioed Kinkaid: "Am proceeding north with three groups to attack enemy carrier force at dawn."

With this message, Halsey intended to turn over the entire defense of the beachhead to Kinkaid and the Seventh Fleet - but Kinkaid thought it meant something very different. Earlier that day, he had picked up a message Halsey sent out about assembling Task Force 34, made up of the big new battleships then serving as escorts for his Task Force 38 carriers, in case of a surface battle. But the message was somewhat garbled, and Kinkaid understood that this was what Halsey *had* done, not what he *might* do. So when Halsey announced that he was going north with "three groups," Kinkaid believed he was taking with him the three carrier groups of Task Force 38 and leaving behind Task Force 34's battleships to guard San Bernardino Strait, north of Leyte.

Kinkaid had no time to worry about such things that night anyway, for his eyes were on the Southern Force steaming toward Surigao Strait. At 2:30 on the morning of October 25, the two battleships, one heavy cruiser, and four destroyers of this force fell into a deadly trap. As the Japanese ships hurried through the narrow strait in the darkness, they were first harassed by torpedo-firing PT boats, then badly hurt by torpedo-firing destroyers, and finally staggered by a hail of shells from the battleships of the Seventh Fleet.

These battleships were old (the newest of them had been completed in 1921), and they were slow, but there was nothing at all wrong with their big guns. "The devastating accuracy of this gunfire was the most beautiful sight I have ever witnessed," said an American officer. Within minutes, most of the Japanese ships were wrecked and sinking; only the cruiser and two destroyers escaped. For *Maryland, California, West Virginia, Tennessee,* and *Pennsylvania* this was sweet revenge. They had all been at Pearl Harbor on December 7, 1941, and had felt the deadly sting of the Japanese surprise attack. The night action wrecked the Japanese Southern Force, but beyond that, it was the last battleship battle in history. The Battle of Surigao Strait was the swan song of the long-time queen of the sea.

Meanwhile, as the Third Fleet rushed through the night toward Ozawa's Northern Force, Halsey turned over command of the coming battle to Marc Mitscher. At dawn, Mitscher put search planes in the air and soon had his first strike winging northward. His raiders found their quarry off Cape Engaño on Luzon, the northernmost island of the Philippines.

A feeble combat air patrol of Zeros was brushed aside by the Hellcats, and the slaughter began. Helldivers put a string of 1,000-pound bombs into the light carrier *Chitose,* and Avengers hit her with two torpedoes. An hour or so later, she blew up and sank. A destroyer also went down, and the fleet carrier *Zuikaku* took a torpedo hit. "The Japs were steaming in a beautiful screen when we went in," said Don Smith, air group commander of the *Enterprise.* "When we left them they looked like a disorderly mob, and every ship was trailing oil."

Soon, a second strike found Ozawa's "disorderly mob." The carrier *Chiyoda*, catching the brunt of the attack, was hit repeatedly and left dead in the water under a towering column of black smoke. Several cruisers and destroyers were also damaged.

Mitscher relentlessly poured planes into the one-sided battle. A third strike badly damaged the *Zuiho.* But the one the American airmen wanted most was the *Zuikaku,* the only carrier left of the six that had bombed Pearl Harbor. She had fought in all the Pacific carrier battles but Midway, repeatedly escaping destruction by the narrowest of margins, and her planes had helped sink the old *Lexington* and the *Hornet.* Now her luck ran out. "I put my group on the *Zuikaku,* and they really smothered her," reported Commander Hugh Winters of the new *Lexington.* "When the torpedoes hit, a narrow plume of water went high into the air like a fire plug that had been run over by a car." The big carrier was obviously doomed; just before the fourth strike came in, she turned over and plunged to the bottom. Mitscher's planes then finished off the *Zuiho,* and later, U.S. cruisers caught up to the derelict *Chiyoda* and sent her under as well. All four of Ozawa's carriers were gone, but he had achieved his object. The Third Fleet had swallowed the bait. Appropriately enough. Cape Engaño is Spanish for "lure" or "deception."

Shortly after dawn that morning, Admiral Halsey had received a report from Admiral Kinkaid about the nighttime action in Surigao Strait; almost as an afterthought, Kinkaid checked Halsey to see that Task Force 34 was keeping a close watch on San Bernardino Strait. He was astonished by Halsey's reply that the battleships were with him. Then, as Mitscher's planes were demolishing the Northern Force, Halsey received a message from Rear Admiral Clifton Sprague, commander of one of the escort carrier groups in Leyte Gulf, saying that he was being shelled by heavy surface ships. This was followed by a barrage of messages from Kinkaid bluntly calling for help.

The Japanese trap had sprung. After prodding from Admiral Toyoda in Tokyo, Kurita's powerful Center Force had reversed course during the night. Despite the loss of the *Musashi,* Kurita still had her mammoth sister-ship *Yamato*, plus three other battleships and six big 8-inch-gunned cruisers. Finding no U.S. ships blocking his path when he emerged from San Bernardino Strait shortly after midnight, he turned south along the coast of Samar, heading full tilt for Leyte Gulf.

Halsey's Third Fleet carriers were 300 miles to the north and helpless to act in time. Kinkaid's Seventh Fleet battleships were at Surigao Strait to the south, three hours' steaming time away. At the moment, all that stood between Kurita and the beachhead was a flock of little escort carriers.

Sixteen of these Seventh Fleet "jeep" carriers were stationed off Leyte to furnish antisubmarine patrols and to make air strikes against Japanese troops on the island. They were divided into three groups. Taffy 3 (so called because of its radio call sign) was to the north, off Samar; Taffy 2 was in the center, opposite Leyte Gulf; and Taffy 1 was to the south. Each group had a screen of destroyers and small destroyer-escorts.

Most of these CVEs were the result of a mass-production project at the Kaiser shipyard in Vancouver, Washington, where they had been completed at the rate of about one a week. They were small and cramped and decidedly unpleasant in rough weather; new men who came aboard were told that CVE stood for "Combustible, Vulnerable, Expendable." They carried a dozen Avengers and about fifteen Wildcat fighters - the big carriers got all the Hellcats as well as all the glory. Most of the time, their duties were routine and dull, except on the morning of October 25, 1944.

Shortly before 7:00 a.m., as Mitscher's strike planes were winging toward Ozawa's carriers off Cape Engaño, one of Taffy 3's six carriers picked up unidentified vessels on her radar. Then an Avenger pilot on antisubmarine patrol reported a formation of Japanese ships some twenty miles away. Admiral Sprague, Taffy 3 commander, ordered the pilot to double-check his identification. Suddenly there was no need to check. Lookouts saw masts on the horizon, and a few minutes later, huge, bright-red geysers of water erupted just astern of the CVEs. The *Yamato's* first salvo of 18-inch shells, containing red dye so her gunners could spot where they hit, landed with ominous accuracy.

Then the rest of Kurita's heavy ships opened fire. "Wicked salvos straddled *White Plains*," Admiral Sprague said later, "and their colored geysers began to sprout among all the other carriers. . . . yellow and purple, the splashes had a kind of horrid beauty." Sprague ordered a smoke screen and sent all his planes into the air, whether they were armed or not, and radioed for help. Near misses were beginning to cause damage when Taffy 3 found temporary shelter in a rain squall.

Sprague knew he dared not stay long where he was. His CVEs could do less than eighteen knots, and already the Japanese were using their superior speed to send out cruisers and destroyers on each flank. His only chance was to keep retreating toward Leyte Gulf and hope that help came in time. Meanwhile, his screen ships would have to buy him time with a counterattack.

In all of American naval history, there is nothing quite like the charge of Taffy 3's screen. The three destroyers and the four destroyer-escorts boldly took on a Japanese fleet of four battleships, six heavy and two light cruisers, and twelve destroyers. They dodged in and out of rain squalls and their own smoke screens, "chased salvos" (turned toward the shell splashes to be out of the way when the enemy corrected his aim), fired torpedoes, and popped away with their 5-inch guns. They did considerable damage, but more important, they threw Kurita's force into confusion as ships fell out of formation to dodge torpedoes; the *Yamato*, for example, had to reverse course for ten minutes to avoid a spread of torpedoes and never got back into the battle.

The screen, however, took a terrible beating. "Three 14-inch shells from a battleship, followed thirty seconds later by three 6-inch shells from a light cruiser, hit us. It was like a puppy being smacked by a truck," said an officer aboard the destroyer *Johnston*. The destroyer *Hoel* took more than forty hits. But the escorts continued punching away with every gun that would fire, and when the *Johnston* went down at last (one of three screen ships lost), a crewman saw the captain of a nearby Japanese destroyer raise his hand in salute.

This battle off Samar (or as one historian called it, "Jeeps vs. Giants") was remarkable for its free-swinging action and its confusion. All during the counterattack by Sprague's screen, the Japanese ships were being harassed from the air. The planes of Taffy 3 and others now appearing from Taffy 2 dropped bombs and torpedoes and strafed, and when they ran out of ammunition, they bluffed attacks to distract the enemy gunners.

Despite the gallant efforts of the screen and the planes, Taffy 3 was taking hits. The enemy battleships were firing from astern, and the flanking cruisers were beginning to pull even. The *Fanshaw Bay* and the *White Plains* were both caught by shells from the cruisers, while the *Kalinin Bay* was heavily damaged by more than a dozen 8-inch shells and a 16-inch shell from the battleship *Nagato.* Fortunately for the jeeps, the Japanese were firing armor-piercing shells that frequently passed completely through the unarmored vessels without exploding.

The *Gambier Bay* was the hardest hit. Before long, the heavy cruiser Chikuma had closed to point-blank range and was driving salvo after salvo into the little carrier. She answered with her one 5-inch gun, but the sea was pouring into her punctured hull too fast to stem. Shortly after 9:00 a.m., the *Gambier Bay* capsized and sank.

Soon after the *Gambier Bay* went down, with the situation growing more critical by the minute, Admiral Sprague heard his signalman complain in a loud voice, "They're getting away!" Sprague later recalled, "I could not believe my eyes, but it looked as if the whole Japanese fleet was, indeed, retiring. However, it took a whole series of reports from circling planes to convince me. And still I could not get the fact to soak into my battle-numbed brain. At best, I had expected to be swimming by this time."

In all the confusion of battle, Admiral Kurita had lost his grip on events. Even though the uncoordinated but fierce attacks by U.S. planes had crippled three of his cruisers, he had plenty of fire power left; yet Kurita and his officers thought they had tangled with a far more powerful force than just a single escort carrier group. This mistake was due in part to the poor visibility, but it also stemmed from the extreme aggressiveness of the American counterattacks.

Finally, because of radio failure, Ozawa was unable to reach Kurita to tell him that Halsey's big carriers were then attacking his Northern Force. Ozawa's sacrifice of his carriers was in vain, for Kurita failed to act on the opportunity it gave him. Instead, he began to worry about air strikes from the Third Fleet. For three hours after letting Taffy 3 slip away, the Japanese Center Force circled off Samar. Finally, a little after noon, Kurita set course for San Bernardino Strait, through which he had steamed so boldly twelve hours before.

Just then, aboard his flagship the *New Jersey*,

pounding southward through the Philippine Sea 300 miles away, Bill Halsey was mad enough to spit fire. When Kinkaid's demands for help came in the morning, Halsey saw there was nothing he could do in time except order Admiral McCain's TG-1, closest to Leyte Gulf, to strike at the Center Force as quickly as possible. In the meantime, he was determined to close with his battleships and wipe out Ozawa's Northern Force.

In midmorning, however, a message arrived from Admiral Nimitz at Pearl Harbor, who was following closely the action reports: "Where is, repeat, where is Task Force 34? The world wonders." As Halsey later recalled, "I was as stunned as if I had been struck in the face. . . . I snatched off my cap, threw it on the deck, and shouted something that I am ashamed to remember."

For mild-mannered Chester Nimitz to resort to a sarcastic, insulting remark like "the world wonders" about the location of the battleships must mean, Halsey thought, that the situation in Leyte Gulf was desperate. Reluctantly, he ordered course reversed. His battleships were then less than forty-five miles from Ozawa's damaged, milling ships. Ten of them got away, and Halsey's chance for the kind of total victory he had dreamed about since his days at the Naval Academy was gone. As it was, his battleships did not reach San Bernardino Strait in time to catch Kurita either; they never fired a single shell.

Only later did Halsey discover that Nimitz never sent the offending phrase at all. To confuse Japanese Intelligence, messages were sent in code with "padding" - random words or phrases - before or after the main message. In this case, Nimitz's coder carelessly added padding that was logical enough for the radiomen aboard Halsey's flagship to think it was part of the message. According to Halsey, Nimitz "blew up when I told him about it; he tracked down the little squirt and chewed him to bits, but it was too late then . . ."

At any rate, the results of the Battle off Samar clearly added up to an American victory, the fourth in two days. The brilliant fight put up by Taffy 3, and Kurita's flustered actions took Admiral Halsey off the hook. His decision to leave San Bernardino Strait unguarded remains controversial, but arguments about it are of the "what might have happened" variety rather than about what did happen.

Kurita's retreat did not end the ordeal of the Taffies on that eventful morning, however. Several times Taffy 1 was attacked by planes from the Philippines. The American crewmen were startled to see the Japanese pilots deliberately aim their planes in suicide dives at the little carriers. Two of the CVEs were badly damaged by such tactics.

No sooner had Taffy 3 gotten clear of Kurita's warships than it too came under air attack. The

Japanese planes came in too low to be spotted on radar, and then climbed quickly and dived at Sprague's jeeps. Both the *Kalinin Bay* and the *Kitkun Bay*, already holed by Japanese shells, were heavily damaged by suicide planes. The *St. Lo* was hit squarely, the enemy plane ripping through the flight deck to the hangar deck, where its bomb exploded. This set off the CVE's bomb and torpedo magazines. Whole planes and great slabs of the flight deck were tossed high in the air. Thirty minutes later, the *St. Lo* broke in half and slid under the waves.

That night, Kurita made good his retreat through San Bernardino Strait, and on the next two days, U.S. carrier planes closed the action by picking off a number of Japanese cripples trying to escape. The Battle for Leyte Gulf was an overwhelming triumph for the U.S. Navy. Against the loss of the light carrier *Princeton* and Taffy 3's casualties - the CVEs *Gambier Bay* and *St. Lo,* two destroyers, and a destroyer-escort - the Third and Seventh fleets had wrecked the Imperial Japanese Navy. Four aircraft carriers, three battleships, ten cruisers, and nine destroyers had been sunk, and as many more ships damaged.

In spite of the victory, the air attacks on Taffy 1 and Taffy 3 had an ominous quality about them. The enemy pilots had obviously taken off with the intention of never coming back, of deliberately crashing their bomb-laden planes into the vulnerable carriers. If this continued, carrier-men told each other, it could mean undreamed-of trouble for the American offensive in the Pacific.

7
KAMIKAZE!

The fight for Leyte Gulf left the Imperial Navy, once Japan's strongest military force, ruined and broken. Without hesitation, the Japanese warlords then threw the last resource available to them, their nation's young men, into a suicide campaign against the American avalanche sweeping them toward defeat.

There was no rest for the Leyte victors in the closing months of 1944, As Admiral Halsey's carrier forces stood by in support of the Philippines campaign, suicide planes struck in ever-increasing numbers. On October 29, the *Intrepid* was hit. The next day both the *Franklin* and the light carrier *Belleau Wood* had their flight decks badly shattered by crashing Japanese planes. On November 5, the *Lexington* was the target; on the twenty-fifth suicide attacks hit four flattops - *Essex, Hancock*, CVL *Cabot*, and the luckless *Intrepid* again. If this were not trouble enough, Halsey's fleet was caught in a typhoon in December. Three destroyers were overwhelmed by the mountainous seas, and aboard the rolling, pitching carriers some 150 planes were damaged beyond repair, more than were lost in the Battle of Midway.

The Japanese christened their suicide force the Kamikaze Corps, taking the name from a famous event in Japan's history. In the thirteenth century, the island kingdom had been about to fall prey to Mongols from the mainland of Asia when a great typhoon destroyed the invaders' fleet. The grateful Japanese had called the typhoon kamikaze, or "divine wind." Now, in the twentieth century, with Japan again threatened by destruction, a human divine wind was directed at the new invaders.

Vice Admiral Takijiro Onishi organized the Kamikaze Corps for the grimly practical reason that most of his inexperienced fliers in their outclassed planes would die anyway. He reasoned, why not have them serve the war effort by exchanging their lives for enemy ships? Such logic, of course, was hardly enough to make thousands of young men eagerly volunteer to kill themselves. The appeal of the Kamikaze Corps stemmed instead from the Japanese character.

The people of Japan combined an unquestioning loyalty to their emperor and their nation with a general indifference to the value of human life. They believed in "life through death," and so death held no terror for them. U.S. Marines experienced this characteristic time after time as they assaulted Japanese strongholds in the Pacific. Enemy soldiers fought until they could fight no more, then killed themselves rather than surrender. As Admiral Halsey put it: "Americans, who fight to live, find it hard to realize that another people will fight to die.

Letters written by kamikaze pilots before their last missions reflect this same attitude toward life and death. "I shall be a shield for His Majesty and die cleanly," a young pilot wrote in late October of 1944. "I wish that I could be born seven times, each time to smite the enemy." A twenty-two-year-old college graduate wrote in his last letter: "Please do not grieve for me, Mother. It will be glorious to die in action. . . . It is gratifying to live in this world, but living has a spirit of futility about it now. It is time to die. I do not seek reasons for dying. My only search is for an enemy target against which to dive."

Admiral Onishi cynically played upon this willingness to commit mass suicide for emperor and homeland. "The salvation of our country . . . can come only from spirited young men such as you. . . . I shall watch your efforts to the end and report your deeds to the Throne," he told a group of kamikaze pilots on one occasion. The Throne, however, was disturbed by the new tactic. "Was it necessary to go to this extreme?" Emperor Hirohito asked his advisers. Yet he made no attempt to halt the campaign.

The fast, maneuverable Zero fighter, carrying a 500-pound bomb, was the most numerous and effective suicide plane. Often the Japanese provided their doomed airmen with a fighter escort to try and break a path through interceptors guarding the U.S. fleet. Sometimes the attackers came in low to escape radar detection; at other times they approached at high altitude, hoping the speed of their dives would be enough to evade fighters and antiaircraft fire. They made such good use of cloud cover that American sailors came to dread overcast days.

Although suicide pilots attacked every type of American ship, even down to the smallest landing craft, aircraft carriers remained their primary targets. By sinking or crippling a big carrier, a single Japanese could put as many as 100 U.S. warplanes out of action - honor enough for any kamikaze pilot. The attackers were taught to aim for a carrier's elevators as the surest way to cripple it. Early in 1945, a *Yorktown* officer noted in his diary: "On the flight deck, painters are outlining false elevators in red. Even if the kamikazes are deceived into hitting them, I don't know how much we'll save by it."

More important steps than painting false elevators were taken to meet the kamikaze threat, of course. By the end of 1944, most of the big flattops carried some seventy fighters and only thirty Avengers and Helldivers. Veteran Marine squadrons brought their fast, rugged Corsairs aboard to help out the Hellcat pilots'. Already in use was an ingenious proximity fuse, which detonated a shell by electrical impulses when it passed anywhere near an enemy plane, making antiaircraft defenses twice as deadly.

One of the most effective tactics was stationing so-called picket destroyers miles away from the task forces to provide radar warning of approaching enemy planes. American strike forces returning from missions were ordered to fly over these pickets and circle once to be "deloused" - that is, to have Hellcats and Corsairs of the combat air patrol pick off any Japanese planes that were following the raiders back to their carriers.

The Allied Pacific timetable for 1945 called first for the liberation of the rest of the Philippines. Next on the target list was Iwo Jima, an island halfway between the Marianas and Japan, to serve as a haven for B-29s in trouble and as a base for the big bombers' fighter escorts. Then would come Okinawa, 350 miles from Japan, needed as an advance naval and air base for the invasion of the home islands scheduled for November, 1945.

Even though the Imperial Navy was helpless to give battle after Leyte Gulf, it still retained fragments of strength that could be dangerous. The two biggest warships in the world were both Japanese - the battleship *Yamato* and the aircraft carrier *Shinano*. The huge carrier, built on the hull of a *Yamato-class* battleship and completed in November 1944, had an armored steel flight deck underlain with concrete, making her all but bombproof. In the predawn hours of November 29, during a trial run near Tokyo Bay, the *Shinano* was hit by four torpedoes from the U.S. submarine *Archerfish*. The sea poured into the shattered hull, and the *Shinano* capsized and sank without ever having launched or landed a plane. *Yamato* had four months to wait for her fateful meeting with the U.S, Navy.

Early in the new year, Task Force 38 supported the invasion of Luzon, the northernmost island of the Philippines, obediently standing by until the troops were safely ashore. Then Halsey led his fighting Third Fleet into "enemy water," the South China Sea. Flying thousands of sorties, U.S. carrier planes pounded enemy harbors and airfields in Indochina, Formosa, and along the China coast, sinking scores of ships and destroying hundreds of planes. Returning to Ulithi, Halsey ended an eventful tour of duty by turning over command of what again became the Fifth Fleet to Admiral Spruance.

Next on the agenda was Iwo Jima. To perform their usual role of knocking out enemy air power near the invasion site, the U.S. carriers struck at Japan itself. Reinforcements had arrived from United States shipyards, and Admiral Mitscher's Task Force 58 now contained eleven fleet carriers and five light carriers. On February 16 and 17, 1945, Avengers, Helldivers, Corsairs, and Hellcats ranged over Tokyo and other Japanese cities, the first U.S. carrier-borne planes to do so since Jimmy Doolittle's B-25s almost three years before. Aircraft factories were heavily bombed, and American airmen claimed over 500 enemy planes destroyed in the air or on the ground.

The Luzon and Iwo Jima campaigns cost the Navy two light carriers and two destroyers, for the 100 percent perfect defense needed against kamikaze attacks was impossible to achieve. Some fifty ships in the invasion fleets, including the carrier *Ticonderoga*, were damaged by suicide attacks. On February 21, the *Saratoga* took a vicious pounding off Iwo Jima. Two attacking Zeros were shot down so close to the ship that their bombs rammed into the hull and exploded. A third bomb hit the forward part of the flight deck, followed seconds later by a Zero that crashed in nearly the same spot. Another plane dove into the starboard side, exploding on the hangar deck. Two hours later, still fighting her fires and counting her dead, the *Saratoga* was staggered by a 1,600-pound bomb that tore a hole in the flight deck twenty-five feet across. Old Sara was too tough to sink, but her damage was so heavy that she was out of action for three months.

At times, Spruance's Fifth Fleet came under scattered but persistent attacks for days on end. One such ordeal began on March 18, 1945, as Task Force 58 began another series of air strikes on Japan in preparation for the Okinawa invasion.

Before dawn, the bonging of the general-quarters alarm sent crewmen running to their battle stations. Shortly after 7:00 a.m., a Hellcat of the combat air patrol downed an enemy snooper. Half an hour later, a Judy slipped up on the *Enterprise* and released its bomb. It was a perfect hit in the middle of the forward elevator, but the Big E's luck still held - the bomb was a dud and failed to explode. At eight, a twin-engine Frances bomber trying to crash-dive the *Yorktown* was blasted apart by the carrier's gunners. Five minutes later, a second Frances splashed so close alongside the *Intrepid* that flaming debris started small fires on her hangar deck.

Shortly before noon, the Japanese appeared again. Radar picked up enemy planes only a few minutes' flying time away just as the carriers prepared to launch an air strike. With no time to take the planes down to the hangar, deck crews hurriedly disarmed them and rolled their bombs and rockets overboard. Hundreds of antiaircraft guns began to track the intruders.

Aboard the carriers, the 5-inchers blazed away first, empty shell casings spewing out the back of the turrets and rolling and bouncing across the flight decks. Then the rapid-firing 40-mitlimeters joined in with a clatter that sounded to one officer "like a regiment of recruits trying to keep step on an iron stairway." The *Yorktown* and the *Intrepid* were narrowly missed by bombs, and five Japanese planes were splashed. At 3:00 p.m., the enemy finally scored - a Judy hit the *Yorktown's* island with a bomb that killed five men but did not harm the ship's offensive power. It was well after dark when Task Force 58 finally secured from battle stations. Many men had been on duty for sixteen or seventeen hours, living on coffee and sandwiches, and they were punch drunk from tension and fatigue.

The next day, March 19, was worse. Soon after sunrise, a bomb hit the *Wasp*, slashing through three decks before exploding and killing over a hundred men. Within fifteen minutes, however, she had her fires out. At almost the same time the *Wasp* was hit, a Japanese bomber popped out of a cloud and put two 550-pound bombs into the *Franklin*.

"Big Ben" was just about to launch a strike against naval bases in Japan, and her flight and hangar decks were jammed with fully armed, fully fueled planes. As Father Joseph O'Callahan, ship's chaplain, described it, "sudden death was everywhere." Gas tanks, bombs, torpedoes, and rockets blew up in a drumfire of deafening noise, and a great wall of fire swept the length of the hangar deck. An officer aboard the *Yorktown* a dozen miles away saw the *Franklin* drifting "dead in the water, with a tremendous plume of black smoke rising from her deck. Every few seconds there was a gush of fire, and the whole ship quaked. I counted nine explosions before she fell astern, hull down over the horizon."

For more than five hours, the *Franklin* was a hellship. "The hangar deck was one massive blaze, not leaping flames, just one solid mass of fire," recalled Father O'Callahan. "Here and there, like coals of special brilliance, were airplane engines glowing white hot, glaring so intensely that their image hurt the eye and branded the memory forever. No one was alive in the hangar deck. No one could live a moment there."

The Big Ben's men fought the flames with great heroism and skill, and the captain of the light cruiser *Santa Fe* put his ship close alongside and kept her there in spite of the explosions to aid in the fire-fighting. Slowly the fires were conquered; twenty-four hours later the blackened, mangled carrier was heading home under her own power.

The *Franklin* had 724 dead, and 265 hurt. No other American ship ever suffered such fearful casualties and stayed afloat.

The assault on the Big Ben did not end this mid-March Japanese counterattack. In an attempt to make their kamikaze campaign even more destructive, the Japanese developed what they called the Oka flying bomb. This weapon resembled a large torpedo with stubby wings and a small tail and contained a 2,600-pound explosive warhead. Dropped by a "mother" plane, the Oka glided down on its target, its speed boosted to over 500 miles an hour by rockets. The pilot was sealed into his cockpit.

On March 21, two days after the *Franklin* was hit, the Japanese were ready to try out the Oka for the first time. Eighteen twin-engine bombers, each one carrying an Oka, tried to get close enough to Task Force 58 to release their deadly cargoes. Detected on radar, the intruders were ambushed by a swarm of Hellcats; all eighteen of the bombers and their Okas were shot down. The flying bombs later scored some successes, but generally they were a bitter disappointment to the Japanese.

The invasion of Okinawa on April 1, 1945, was supported by an armada of some 1,500 ships, ranging from landing craft to battleships and carriers. Task Force 58, somewhat under strength after its March duels with the kamikazes, received from Britain's Royal Navy a welcome reinforcement of four carriers and their escorts. The British flattops carried fewer planes than Essex-class vessels, but their armored steel flight decks made them stronger defensively. The *Indefatigable* and the *Victorious* were both hit squarely by suicide planes, and the *Formidable* was struck twice, but they were back in action within hours.

The Okinawa assault was the death warrant of the giant battleship *Yamato*. She was sent on a suicide dash toward the beachhead with only enough fuel oil in her tanks for a one-way trip. Nearly 400 of Admiral Mitscher's carrier planes found the *Yamato* long before she reached Okinawa and pursued her like hounds after a stag. Helldivers left the battleship's superstructure a shambles, and a half-dozen torpedo hits caused her to list sharply to port. Lieutenant Thomas Stetson, leading the *Yorktown's* Avengers, saw the thick belt of protective armor on the starboard side high out of the water. "Hit her in the belly - now!" he ordered his pilots. Five torpedoes ripped into the exposed hull under the armor belt. Slowly the great ship rolled over, her magazines exploding as she sank.

The Okinawa campaign cost the Americans 763 planes and the Japanese ten times that number. Thirty U.S. ships were sunk, more than 100 were badly damaged, and nearly 5,000 sailors lost their lives, most of them to the kamikazes. "At the end of each day, canvas shrouds slipped into the waters off Okinawa," wrote Admiral Mitscher's biographer of those bloody, tense, exhausting weeks. "Death was in the air and on the face of the sea. The Divine Wind blew hot and steadily."

The radar picket destroyers received as much attention from the suicide pilots as the carriers. The destroyer *Laffey,* for example, was hit by no less than six kamikazes and four bombs in one day, but she survived. With grim humor, the crewmen of one of these pickets painted on her deck a huge arrow pointing off to the side, and beneath it, they added in large letters, "Carriers that way!"

On April 16, the hard-luck *Intrepid* was hit again. (She had been damaged so often and spent so much time in drydock for repairs, that she was known throughout the fleet as the Dry I and the Decrepid.) On May 11, it was the *Bunker Hill's* turn. "One minute our task force was cruising in lazy circles about 60 miles off Okinawa . . ." wrote a war correspondent. "The next the *Bunker Hill* was a pillar of flame. It was as quick as that - like summer lightning." A Zero and a Judy hit Admiral Mitscher's flagship at almost the same instant, just as she was launching an air strike. The result was horribly similar to what had happened to the *Franklin.* Over 350 men died before the inferno was conquered.

Admiral Mitscher transferred his flag to the *Enterprise,* but three days later the Big E's fabled luck finally ran out. A Zero with a 500-pound bomb under its fuselage ducked out of a cloud and raced in on the carrier from astern. Directly over the flight deck the enemy pilot flipped his plane over on its back and dived into the deck. The bomb plunged into the forward elevator well and exploded, blowing the elevator 400 feet into the air. Damage control quickly had matters in hand, but the *Enterprise's* war career was over.

The Allied forces shook off these casualties and pushed on. Germany had surrendered on May 7, and Japan was clearly failing fast. In June, Okinawa was secured, and work proceeded swiftly to turn the island into a springboard for the invasion of Japan. In July and August, the Third Fleet, with Halsey again in command, ranged up and down the Japanese coast sowing destruction. Superfortresses from the Marianas demolished factories and rained death on the crowded cities. Undaunted, the warlords hoarded their remaining planes for a massive kamikaze counterattack on the invasion forces expected soon.

But on August 6, a B-29 from Tinian wiped out the city of Hiroshima with an atomic bomb. Three days later a second bomb destroyed Nagasaki. On August 15, with his fighters and bombers on the way to Tokyo, Admiral Halsey received the order to cease fire. Japan had surrendered unconditionally. "The guns are silent," General MacArthur said in a radio broadcast to the American people. "A great tragedy has ended. A great victory has been won. The skies no longer rain death - the seas bear only commerce men everywhere walk upright in the sunlight . . ."

The atomic bombs wrote a dramatic finish to the war in the Pacific, but it was the aircraft carrier, more than any other single weapon, that had made final triumph possible. From the first check to Japan's Pacific advance in the Coral Sea in 1942 through the turning of the tide at Midway and Guadalcanal, they stood virtually alone against the might of the Imperial Japanese Navy. The spectacular carrier victory in the Battle of the Philippine Sea insured the conquest of the Marianas and brought Japan within range of the B-29s - and eventually within range of atomic holocaust. Leyte Gulf, in large part a carrier action, signaled the death of a navy that for a time had been the most powerful in the world.

In between these battles, the flattops proved time and again their hitting power, beating down Japanese resistance on the ground, at sea, and in the air in their coverage of dozens of amphibious landings. New carriers and new carrier planes, refinements of fighting tactics, unfailing brilliance of leadership - all combined to beat Japan to its knees faster than anyone would have believed possible in those grim days early in 1942.

The aircraft carrier's offensive might, its elusiveness, its ability to furnish "instant" air power in any corner of the seven seas have proved equally valuable in the Cold War crises of the postwar era. Sometimes the mere presence of carriers has deterred conflict;

on other occasions, as in the Korean War in the early 1950s and in Vietnam in the mid-1960s, they have proved their worth when America found it necessary to fight Communist aggression.

Many of the carriers that did so much to achieve victory against Japan have been modernized and still serve the Navy. The *Essex*, for example, is an ASW (Anti-Submarine Warfare) vessel, while the *Lexington* serves as a training ship for new pilots. Their place on the battle line has been taken by supercarriers armed largely with jet-powered, supersonic planes.

Two other historic fighting ships, however, are no more. The gallant *Saratoga* ended a twenty-year career the victim of a postwar atomic test. The *Enterprise* was denied the dignity of a death at sea. In 1945, Secretary of the Navy James Forrestal called the Big E the "one vessel that most nearly symbolizes the history of the Navy in this war" and proposed that she be preserved alongside the *Constitution* and the *Constellation,* heroic American frigates from the age of sail. Forrestal's suggestion was fitting for between December 7, 1941, and May 14, 1945, the *Enterprise* compiled a fighting record unmatched by any warship in history. But no money for her preservation came from the government, and a public fund-raising drive led by Admiral Halsey fell short. In 1959, the Big E was scrapped.

Yet her name and her fighting spirit did not die. Even as the shipbreakers went about their work, wrote the *Enterprise's* historian, "a colossal structure was growing in a graving dock at Newport News, Virginia, not far from the ways where the Big E was launched twenty-three years before. . . . Early in 1961 the dock was flooded, and *Enterprise*, the first nuclear carrier in history, the biggest ship in the world, again the pride of her country and its Navy, first felt the touch of the sea. The story of the Big E had begun again."

27391317R00101

Printed in Great Britain
by Amazon